let your LIGHT SHINE

Other Soul Deep Scripture Journals
from *Sweet To The Soul Ministries*

31-Day Scripture Journals:

New Life

Love Is

Grace

God's Masterpiece

I Believe

7-Day Scripture Journals:

Together We're Better

Rest for the Weary Soul

Downloadable Journal formats available at:

SweetToTheSoul.com/SoulDeep

All proceeds from the sale of *Soul Deep Devotionals and Journals*
go toward providing Bible Study Materials to women incarcerated and in shelters.

let your Light Shine

Being A Light In A Dark World

A 31 - Day Soul Deep Devotional and Journal

Let Your Light Shine : Being a Light in a Dark World
A 31 Day Soul Deep Devotional
Copyright © 2016 by Sweet To The Soul Ministries
All rights reserved.
www.SweetToTheSoul.com

Illustrations: Copyright © 2016 Jana Kennedy-Spicer
Cover Design by: Jana Kennedy-Spicer
Interior Design by: Jana Kennedy-Spicer

ISBN-13: 978-1537560502

ISBN-10: 1537560506

No part of this publication may be reproduced, distributed, or transmitted in any form or by any means, including photocopying, recording, or other electronic or mechanical methods, without the prior written permission of the publisher, except in the case of brief quotations embodied in critical reviews and certain other noncommercial uses permitted by copyright law. For inquiries and permission request, contact through website: www.SweetToTheSoul.com

CreateSpace Independent Publishing Platform, North Charleston, SC

Unless otherwise noted, all scripture quotations are taken from The Holy Bible, English Standard Version ("ESV®") Copyright © 2001 by Crossway, a publishing ministry of Good News Publishers. Used by permission. All rights reserved. ESV Text Edition: 2011

Scripture quotations marked NIV are taken from The Holy Bible: NEW INTERNATIONAL VERSION, NIV Copyright © 1973, 1978, 1984, 2011 by Biblicia, Inc. Used by permission. All rights reserved worldwide.

Scripture quotations marked NASB are taken from the New American Standard Bible®, ("NASB") Copyright © 1960, 1962, 1963, 1968, 1971, 1972, 1973, 1975, 1977, 1995 by The Lockman Foundation Used by permision." (www.Lockman.org)

Scripture quotations marked HCSB®, are taken from the Holman Christian Standard Bible®, Copyright © 1999, 2000, 2002, 2003, 2009 by Holman Bible Publishers. Used by permission. HCSB® is a federally registered trademark of Holman Bible Publishers.

Scripture quotations marked NLT are taken from the Holy Bible, New Living Translation, copyright ©1996, 2004, 2007, 2013, 2015 by Tyndale House Foundation. Used by permission of Tyndale House Publishers, Inc., Carol Stream, Illinois 60188. All rights reserved.

To Nita.
Always and forever a beautiful reflection of God's light.

*Thank you for letting your light shine into my life and the lives
of so many others.*

*"And we all, with unveiled face, beholding the glory of the Lord,
are being transformed into the same image from one degree of glory to another.
For this comes from the Lord who is the Spirit."*
2 Corinthians 3:18

Contents:

Introduction	ix
Color Sheet—Matthew 5:14	xxi
Day 01 Matthew 5:14-16	1
Day 02 Job 33:28	7
Day 03 Psalm 4:6	13
Day 04 Romans 13:12	19
Bible Study —Word Study	24
Day 05 John 8:12	26
Day 06 Isaiah 60:19	32
Color Sheet—Shine so other see Christ	38
Day 07 Revelation 21:24	39
Day 08 Psalm 119:130	45
Day 09 1 Thessalonians 5:5	51
Day 10 Micah 7:9	57
Color Sheet—Let Your Light Shine	63
Day 11 Matthew 6:22	64
Day 12 Psalm 18:28	70
Day 13 Isaiah 60:1	76
Day 14 Acts 13:47	82
Bible Study —Bible Study Tools	88
Day 15 Ephesians 5:13	90
Day 16 Psalm 97:11	96
Day 17 Job 24:13	102
Day 18 Isaiah 2:5	109
Color Sheet—Psalm 119:105	114

Day 19 1 John 1:5	115
Day 20 Psalm 36:9	121
Bible Study — Verse Mapping	126
Day 21 2 Corinthians 4:6	130
Day 22 1 Peter 2:9	136
Day 23 Isaiah 42:16	142
Day 24 Psalm 43:3	148
Color Sheet — John 12:36	154
Day 25 John 12:35	149
Day 26 Luke 11:33	161
Color Sheet — John 1:5	167
Day 27 John 1:5	168
Day 28 2 Corinthians 11:14	174
Day 29 Psalm 56:13	180
Day 30 Isaiah 9:2	186
Color Sheet — Candle Light	192
Day 31 Revelation 22:5	193
Bonus Section: Praying Scripture	201
Things to Remember	215
Meet Our Contributors	223
Additional Resources	233
Free Gifts For You	
Join Our Community	

Introduction

For awhile now, I've been praying the same prayer, every day.

Lord, create in me a desire for Your Word. Amen

It's short. It's simple. *But it's soul deep*. And it's a prayer, I feel, God finds joy in answering.

So earlier this year, I put together a study journal for my own personal use. It was simple. I wanted to read and study the scriptures, to dive in, to sit with God and have this conversation with Him through His Word. But the whole 'open your Bible and start reading' approach didn't really work for me. I just didn't know where to start.

So I prayed about a topic. When I asked God where to start, what He wanted to talk about, He answered right away and in a big way. With not just one topic, not even two or three. He didn't answer with some rain drops, he answered with a flood! I think I have monthly study topics to last a few years. When I asked God what He wanted to talk about, He filled up my calendar.

Now I would love to invite you to join me on this Soul Deep journey. Oh I am so hungry for The Word of God. I, just like all of the ladies joining in this project, am happy to share with you, with anyone who will listen, how God has shown up in our lives and what He has taught us through His Word.

My prayer for you, is the same prayer I began with. For God to create a desire in your heart for His Word. You see, I know if you have that desire, He will more than satisfy your hunger. He longs to have relationship with us, to spend time together, to reveal Himself to us. I have found in my life when there has been a distance between God an myself, it is because I have placed span between us; He is standing faithful waiting for me to return.

The topic we will be diving into with this devotional is: *Light*.

We live in a dark world, and it seems to be getting darker day by day. Fear, depression, grief, abuse, illness can seem overwhelming. But there is hope. *There is a light*.

We want the world to know *who* is the light, and we want to know Him better.

Lord, create in me a desire for Your Word. AMEN

> "And Jesus spoke to them saying, 'I am the *light of the world.* Whoever follows me will not walk in darkness, but will have the light of life.'" ~ John 8:12

I love this topic and look forward to diving soul deep into the scriptures with you.

I have invited several of my Soul Friends along on this journey. Each will be sharing from their personal experiences and talking with us about the insight they received from studying these scriptures about light. What I love so much about having such a variety of friends joining in, is how the message from each individual scripture unfolds for them personally, and for you as well. The beauty of so many of us reading, studying, writing and sharing about the same topic and scriptures, is that God speaks to each of us individually and personally, and reveals exactly what we need to hear from Him.

Scattered throughout this devotional journal, you will also find Bible study tips and information about study resources. There are pages to color and plenty of room to journal and study creatively, so let your soul be inspired. I love to color in my Bible and write and highlight all over the books I read. So I hope when you've finished *Let Your Light Shine*, it is used up, marked over and dog-eared.

This is a devotional to use **with** your Bible not **instead of** your Bible. Open it up, and open your Bible. Linger there. Pray there. Meet God there. And then write down what He said, make notes of the moments you shared.

And then ... Tell somebody. Come tell us. Join our community on-line and share with us what God has revealed to you through spending time with Him in His Word.

I normally wouldn't suggest that someone start a book at the back of the book, but that's where I'm going to suggest you go before you ever begin with Day 1. In the back of this book I want to show you these sections.

- **Praying Scripture**. I believe prayer is a vital part of Bible study, so a bonus section just about prayer has been included. I invite you to go there first, where you will find blank prayer journal pages as well as a daily prayer prompt to use during your study time each day.

- **Meet Our Contributors**. Joining me on this soul deep study journey are several of my Soul Friends with the most beautiful hearts for Jesus. In this section, you can learn more about each one and find out how to personally connect with each contributor.

- **Additional Resources**. Flip a few more pages over and you will find a section listing all of the additional resources we offer which compliment this devotional. In addition, there are several free downloads which can be used in conjunction with *Let Your Light Shine*.

But the aspect of this devotional and journal I am most excited about is such a blessing.

For every copy of *Let Your Light Shine* purchased, a woman incarcerated in prison or living in a shelter will receive a copy of *Let Your Light Shine* for free.

Yes, free.

> *All proceeds* from the sale of Soul Deep devotionals, journals and other materials,
> go towards providing Soul Deep Bible study materials *free of charge*
> to women incarcerated in prison or living in a shelter.
>
> At the heart of Sweet To The Soul Ministries is the desire to share God's Word with women.
> To Encourage the Study of God's Divinely Inspired Word.

So thank you for partnering with us in ministry and blessing other women with these Bible study materials.

Soul Friends, I so look forward to this study journey with you. And I pray that God reveal His light to you in life changing ways.

Blessings,

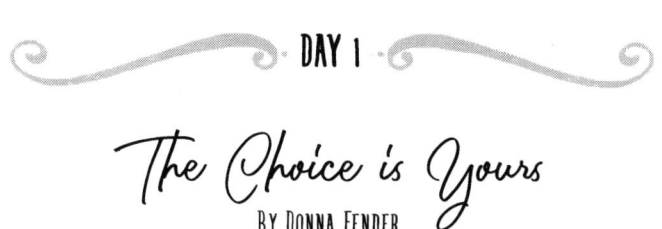

DAY 1

The Choice is Yours
By Donna Fender

> "YOU ARE THE LIGHT OF THE WORLD,
> A CITY SET ON A HILL CANNOT BE HIDDEN."
> MATTHEW FIVE : FOURTEEN

"I don't like to fly" she exclaimed. "Well, the good news is that you don't have to fly because I am the one who is going on the trip", I replied. The time came and as we stood in the airport waiting for me to board the plane a familiar statement rang in my ears. "Remember who you are and Who you represent."

Who do we represent? What a loaded question.

I grew up in church, singing all the Bible songs and being told that there was a God who was real and would take care of all my needs. I learned when I was young that I had a light inside of me that was there to shine for the whole world to see. But if you are reading this, you may not have a clue what shining a light means....*especially when it means that you are shining it for Jesus.*

So, what does shining a light mean?

We must first understand *who* the Light is.

In John 8:12 we read, "*Jesus spoke to them saying 'I am the Light of the world. Whoever follows me will not walk in darkness, but will have the light of life."* (ESV).

Jesus is the Light. Jesus gives us life and when we accept His offer to follow Him, we have His light in us to share for all to see.

When we make the choice to decline His offer, we continue to live in darkness and are lost. In other words, we have something missing and will continue to look around in every aspect of our lives to fill the void....*with no success*, I might add.

Without Jesus, we become a reflection of the world.

So, until we follow Jesus and accept His free gift of life everlasting, we cannot shine His light. God chases us and graces us with Himself and we could not ask for anything more. when we decide to be a Jesus follower we can then learn from our focus verses how to shine for Him.

Matthew 5:14-16 says this: *"You are the light of the world. A city set on a hill cannot be hidden. Nor do people light a lamp and put it under a basket, but on a stand, and it gives light to all in the house. In the same way, let your light shine before others, so that they may see your good works and give glory to your Father in Heaven."* (ESV)

Basically, we become a reflection of the One who brings light to our life. We need to stand high, not being ashamed of the light we have been given. When others ask why we shine, we are able to share that it is because Jesus lives in us. With Jesus, we become a reflection of Him.

Living in Jesus offer true freedom and we become a reflection of His love and perfection.

What does your reflection look like?
- The brightness of His Light or the absence of His light.
- Do you follow the world or do you follow Jesus?

We have a choice and we can choose to represent the Light or the dark.

Choosing to follow Jesus is not as complicated as we think. We must simply believe and accept His invitation.

Read the following verses to learn what Jesus has done for you and me!

- Romans 3:23, *"for all have sinned and fall short of the glory of God,"* (NIV)
- Romans 6:23, *"For the wages of sin is death, but the free gift of God is eternal life in Christ Jesus our Lord."* (ESV)
- Romans 5:8, *"but God shows his love for us in that while we were still sinners, Christ died for us."* (ESV)
- Romans 10:13, *"For everyone who calls on the name of the Lord will be saved."* (ESV)
- Romans 10:9-10, *"if you confess with your mouth that Jesus is Lord and believe in your heart that God raised him from the dead, you will be saved. For with the heart one believes and is justified, and with the mouth one confesses and is saved."* (ESV)

What's your choice?

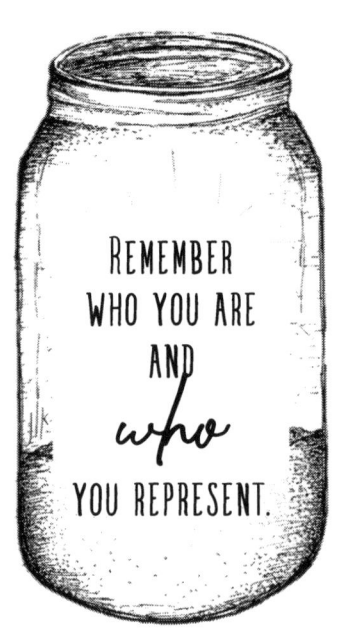

Read:

1. Read John 1:5. *"The light shines in the darkness, and the darkness has not overcome it."* (ESV)

    Is there darkness in your life? Declare what is dark in your life and ask God to bring His light in the darkest corners of your life.

    God loves you and me so much and want us to be His reflections for all to see.

2. Read John 10:10. *"The thief comes only to steal and kill and destroy. I came that they may have life and have it abundantly."* (ESV)

    Jesus wants to offer us a life of abundance, why not represent Him and all that He offers? What does it look like to represent God?

    If it was your last day on earth, who or what would people say that you represent?

    Let's be women who know who we are and Who we represent!

Reflect and Relate:

1. With Jesus we reflect Him....even in our brokenness. We are all broken, even those of us who "grew up in church." Your story can be re-written with a different ending when we let Jesus write our story. Read John 3:30. *"He must increase, but I must decrease."* (ESV)

    When we decrease so God can increase, our story becomes less about what happened to us and more about what God did to rescue and redeem us. How does this perspective re-write your story?

2. Have you ever shared your story with another? If not, practice reminding yourself what God has done in your life. Journal some notes. Then ask a friend if you can practice sharing your story with them.

    Start here: What words describe you now after God has rewritten your story.

Prayer:

Dear Lord, I pray for each woman who will receive and read this devotion on Light. Lord, thank you for shining so bright in a dark, dark world so that we may have hope. Lord, help us to understand that even in our brokenness that we can still shine Your light but if we do not know you, we are trapped in a life of darkness. Lord, I pray that we accept your invitation and choose You! In Jesus' name, Amen.

Prayer Journal

Prompt: For boldness to be a witness for Christ

Praise:

For Others:

For Me:

Thanksgiving:

Let Your Soul Be Inspired

DAY 2

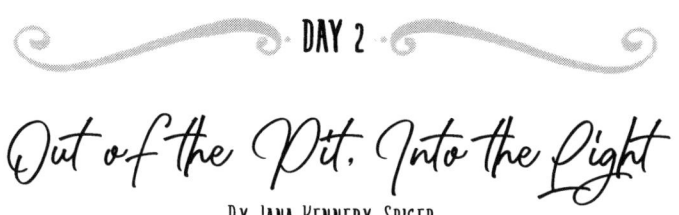

Out of the Pit, Into the Light
By Jana Kennedy-Spicer

> "He has redeemed my soul from going down into the pit, and my life shall look upon the light."
>
> Job thirty-three : twenty-eight

I'd like to introduce you to Job. A man God Himself called, "*blameless and upright ... God fearing ... turns from evil.*" Job 1:8 (ESV)

You may already know Job, but if not, let me fill you in on his story.

Here's Job, an upright Godly man and successful by any standard: large family, huge home with a lot of property, great numbers of livestock, many employees, wealthy and high standing in the community; then one day the enemy (devil) comes along and wants to test Job's faithfulness to God, so he takes it all away. **ALL. OF. IT.** When this doesn't shake Job's faith, the enemy then makes Job painfully ill.

Very quickly Job went from king of the hill to down and out in the valley.

Have you ever been there? I sure have, on top of the world one moment, then buried below what once was my life the very next. If you find yourself there right now friend, keep reading, there is *hope*.

At Job's lowest point, his friends, who try to help, end up accusing him of bringing all these hardships on himself by rebelling against God.

Now, we have an advantage here, because if we read the book of Job, we have the narrative and full picture, we know what is really going on. But Job and his friends did not. All Job knows is that all of these really bad things are happening to him but he has no idea as to why.

This is where I typically find myself when difficulties occur – in the midst of the storm but not knowing exactly where it came from.

The storms of life are a test of our faith. Will they overtake us? Will our faith be stronger than the powerful winds of turmoil and tragedy?

When taking his family, possessions, status and health did not knock Job off of his firm foundation [God], the enemy launched an attack on his mind. And oh what a battle ground! Shame, regret, bitterness, pride, doubt – these are just a few of the destructive weapons the enemy uses as he attacks our minds.

How did this impact Job? *"Let the stars of its dawn be dark. Let it hope for light but have none, nor see the eyelids of the morning."* Job 3:9 (ESV)

Job began to lose confidence in God, to see himself as no value to God, to lament his very birth and he didn't want to see the light of another day. Job found himself is such a deep dark pit of despair.

But God ... loves us and intervenes for us.

Today's scripture mentions a mediator, "He", someone who intercedes on one's behalf and makes peace, or offers a solution. We have a tremendous mediator intervening on our behalf – Jesus!

> ***"For God so loved the world, that he gave his only Son, that whoever believes in him should not perish but have eternal life."*** John 3:16 (ESV)

He offers to rescue us from the eternal pit of despair – hell – and deliver us into the eternal splendor of life with God, "the light."

I say he "offers" this to us, because we have the choice to decide to receive this redemption or to reject Him. We are offered a way out of the pit, but we have to take it. We must confess and repent of our sins, reach out and take God's hand offering salvation.

"It was for my welfare I had great bitterness, but in love you have delivered my life from the pit of destruction, for you have cast my sins behind your back." Isaiah 68:17 (ESV)

Oh what a joyous day! When God brings us out of the dark pit and into His light.

So what happened to Job? God came to him – you see, God meets us where we are, even if we're in a deep dark pit; Job answered God and repented for his lack of faith; and God brought restoration to Job's life.

"And the Lord blessed the latter days of Job more than the beginning..." Job 42:12a (ESV)

Read:

1. Read Psalm 40:2, *"He drew me up from the pit of destruction, out of the murky bog, and set my feet upon a rock making my steps secure."* (ESV)

   List what Psalm 40:2 tells us God can do for us?

   Rewrite the verse below, personalizing it by changing "me/my" to your name.

2. Read 1 Timothy 2:5-6, *"For there is one God and one mediator between God and mankind, the man Christ Jesus, who gave himself as a ransom for all people..."* (ESV)

   What are your sins which were nailed to the cross with Jesus when he paid the ransom for you?

Reflect and Relate:

1. We all find ourselves in a pit at some point in our lives, maybe even over and over again. What pit have you been in, or are in right now?

    In Psalm 40:2, the psalmist describes their pit as a murky (dark, gloomy, unclear, confused) bog (muck, quicksand, swamp). In what way(s) did / does your pit feel the same?

2. Job 42:12 tells us that God blessed Job's latter years – after his confession, repentance and restoration – more than the years before.

    If you have accepted God's gift of redemption and restoration, in what ways has He blessed your life after?

Prayer:

Dear Lord, oh thank you for lifting me up out of the pit – time and time again. Forgive me of my doubt and lack of faith when storms hit. Strengthen me and remind me of your faithfulness! Thank you for providing a firm foundation for my feet. Guide me as I go through each day to stay on the path you have laid out for me, helping me to avoid the hidden pits dug out by the enemy. In Jesus' holy name, Amen.

Prompt: For those suffering through hardships

Praise:

For Others:

For Me:

Thanksgiving:

Let Your Soul Be Inspired

DAY 3

What's the World Coming To
By Cathy Chung

> "THERE ARE MANY WHO SAY, 'WHO WILL SHOW US SOME GOOD? LIFT UP THE LIGHT OF YOUR FACE UPON US, O LORD!'"
>
> PSALM FOUR : SIX

My grandmother shook her head over rising skirt lengths. My mother was exasperated by modern lyrics. I, too, have wondered where we're headed when I watch the evening news.

We live in a world that doesn't follow God.

Some question why God allows the suffering we see from today's poverty and injustice. They mock "Where is God?" when natural disasters destroy lives or terrorists attack innocents. Some laugh at us for believing biblical nonsense. Some seek happiness in social status and possessions.

It's as hard for Christians today as it was for the psalmist of Old Testament times.

When he wrote Psalm 4, King David was distressed that the Israelite's faith was wavering. They had suffered greatly and questioned God's faithfulness. They sought other gods in an attempt to improve their lives.

Though frustrated by the culture, David confidently proclaimed
      "You can be sure of this: the Lord will answer when I call to Him." Psalm 4:3 (NLT)
Then he asked for God's presence,
      "Let the light of your face shine upon us, O Lord." Psalm 4:6 (NIV)

While surrounded by the same kind of discouraging circumstances we face today, David asked God to come near – close enough for the light from God's face to shine on him. He needed reassurance that he wasn't alone. *He didn't ask God to change the world, just to be present.*

And God answered David's prayer. Can you imagine it? God's hands firmly hold David's shoulders as their foreheads touch tenderly - the Father pouring strength into his son. "Don't be afraid. I'm right here."

Do we share David's confidence that God hears our cries and answers our prayers?

What could we gain if we realized God's presence is available any time we ask?

With my powerful God close by, I'd certainly stand taller because together we could handle anything. I'd have a personal tutor for understanding scripture and a clearer distinction between right and wrong. With God next to me, I might have unusual courage (maybe even supernatural courage) to step out of my comfort zone and to resist temptation. If I felt discouraged or sad, His presence would offer hope and comfort.

It sounds pretty awesome, doesn't it?

Here's the amazing thing. We can be as confident as David because Jesus promised to send a Counselor, the Holy Spirit, who would take up residence in every believer. Jesus said:

"[The Father] will give you another Counselor to be with you forever – the Spirit of truth. If anyone loves me, he will obey my teaching. My Father will love him, and we will come to him and make our home with him. But the Counselor, the Holy Spirit, will teach you all things and will remind you of everything I have said to you." John 14:16-17 (NIV) emphasis added

"But you will receive power when the Holy Spirit comes on you; and you will my witnesses...to the ends of the earth." Acts 1:8 NIV emphasis added

Jesus said *"we (meaning God and Jesus) will come and make our home"* with those who love God. This is the Holy Spirit that lives in you and lives in me, empowering us with His constant presence. If we tap into its power, the result (or fruit) will be *"love, joy, peace, patience, kindness, goodness, faithfulness, gentleness and self-control"* Galatians 6:22 (NIV)

> THE WORLD DOESN'T CHANGE, BUT WE CAN HAVE CONFIDENCE TO FACE LIFE'S CHALLENGES BY *trusting* GOD.

Sure, we already possess some of these characteristics. Through our own effort we can sometimes be patient, but then our tempers flare. We often show kindness, but not to everyone. When we allow the Holy Spirit to come alive in us, we are transformed into His likeness and see people and situations through Jesus' eyes.

The world doesn't change, but we can have confidence to face life's challenges, courage to hold firm to our values, patience to withstand attacks on our faith, inner joy through unhappy times, hope that God has a bigger plan than we can know, kindness for our enemies, love for those whose opinions differ, and self-control in the face of worldly temptations. *By trusting God, we find peace.*

Read:

1. Read 2 Corinthians 3:18: *"So all of us who have had that veil removed can see and reflect the glory of the Lord, and the Lord, who is the Spirit, makes us more and more like Him as we are changed into His glorious image."* (NLT)

    What is the veil that stands between you and God?

    What does the Spirit do when the veil is removed?

2. Read Romans 12:2: *"Don't copy the behavior and customs of this world, but let God transform you into a new person by changing the way you think. Then you will learn to know God's will for you, which is good and pleasing and perfect."* (NLT)

    According to this verse, how will God's Spirit transform you into a new person?

Reflect and Relate:

1. What challenge do you face today?

2. Look at the situation through Jesus' eyes. How can the Spirit living inside you help change the way you think about and approach the situation?

3. How does knowing God is with you help you face this challenge?

Prayer:

Dear God, Thank you for your constant presence through the Holy Spirit. Living in today's culture can be confusing and discouraging because its ways are so far from your Truth. May your Spirit transform us into people who see through your eyes and reflect your character. In the name of our Savior Jesus Christ, Amen.

Prompt: For God to open the door to be an encouragement to someone

Praise:

For Others:

For Me:

Thanksgiving:

Let Your Soul Be Inspired

DAY 4

A New Wardrobe
By Jana Kennedy-Spicer

> "The night is far gone; the day is at hand. So then let us cast off the works of darkness and put on the armor of light."
>
> Romans Thirteen : Twelve

Our family loves amateur sports. Almost all of the grandkids, which are old enough, participate on some type of team. One is a dancer, two play baseball, two more play football, another plays basketball and one is a cheerleader. Boys and girls alike, they all play sports. And almost every weekend a similar scene plays out....

> A game is played, then the jersey wearing warriors pile in the car to head home, or maybe to get ice cream with Nana and Paw Paw.

After one game, the grandsons belted themselves in to their mom's car then one proclaimed, "Mom, your car stinks!" To which she replied, "It's not my car, it's the two of you!"

She learned after that first game to take the footballers a change of clothes so they could shed the dirty foul smelling uniforms and put on fresh clean clothes before gathering in her car.

Just like these kids needed to shed their dirty clothes, we are also called to "cast off" the works of the darkness and "put on" the armor of light.

In Paul's letter to the church in Rome, he covers many topics. In today's scripture, he is encouraging the church to cast off or cease their sinful actions and put on the armor of light to fight the spiritual battle of temptation. He also uses a similar example in his letter to the Christians living in the small city of Colossae.

In Colossians chapter 3 we are taught that because, as Christians, we have spiritually died to our old self and have been reborn in Christ, we are to "put to death what is earthly" (vs 5). We then find in verses 5-9 a list of examples of the "works of darkness" we are to shed, or take off.

The imagery here is that we have these actions and attitudes which we wear. And just like we select what clothes we are going to wear each day, we also select which actions and attitudes to wear – will they be sinful, of the darkness, or glorifying to God, of the light?

Paul is telling us it is time to clean out our closets. To get rid of all of those old sinful ways, to toss them so we don't even have the option to wear them again. It's like spring cleaning in the closet of our heart.

The word he uses for "cast off" is strong. It means more than just removing them, but to renounce or disown them, to give them up entirely, to reject them. That is a lot more permanent than just switching our wardrobe out for a season.

Every so often, but not near enough, I clean out our closet and remove the clothes no longer worn so they can be donated for someone else to love. But there always remains this one section of t-shirts. Most are old and worn, and I no longer wear them, but they carry some good memories.

Just like our home closets need to be regularly cleaned out, so do our heart closets.

Maybe we've welcomed in a new sinful attitude. That sweater of bitterness is starting to be something that we live in. Or maybe it's not anything new at all. Maybe we keep hanging on to that old t-shirt of rejection and hurt feelings. We don't wear it every day but some days we take it out just to look at it and remember.

Paul understands that if we cast off these, then we need to put on something else, because he doesn't leave us spiritually naked. After we remove "the works of darkness" he encourages us to put on "the armor of the light." We need to suit up in the weapons we need for our daily spiritual warfare. In Ephesians 6:10-18, we are given the full list of spiritual armor God provides for us to wear into battle.

But, right now, let's take a look at the actions and attitudes we need to switch out in our spiritual wardrobe.

> *"Put to death therefore what is earthly in you: sexual immorality, impurity, passion, evil desire, and covetousness, which is idolatry. But now you must put them all away: anger, wrath, malice, slander, and obscene talk from your mouth."* Colossians 3:5, 8-9 (ESV)

> *"Put on then, as God's chosen ones, holy and beloved, compassionate hearts, kindness, humility, meekness, and patience, bearing with one another and, if one has a complaint against another, forgiving each other; as the Lord has forgiven you, so you also must forgive. And above all these put on love, which binds everything together in perfect harmony."*
> Colossians 3:12-14 (ESV)

Did you notice when reading through those lists that each action or attitude directly impacts how we relate to each other, to fellow Christians and to those outside of our faith?

We are told several times in scripture that to unbelievers, the children of God will be known by their actions. In John 13:35, *"By this all people will know you are my disciples, if you have love for one another."* (ESV) and Titus 1:16, *"They profess to know God, but deny Him by their works. They are detestable, disobedient, unfit for any good work."* (ESV)

Just like the players on my grandson's football team are recognized by their uniforms, so are Christians recognized by what we wear, *by the external expression of our internal spiritual wardrobe*. Do we wear the sins of darkness or the light of new life in God?

I think it may be time to clean some old things out of my spiritual closet, to let in the light. How about you?

Diving Deeper

Read:

1. Read again Colossians 3:5-9, on the previous page. Circle the actions and attitudes we are to cast off.

   List those that you might have a difficult time casting off.

2. Read again Colossians 3:12-14, on the previous page. Circle the actions and attitudes we are to put on.

   List those that you might have a difficult time putting on.

Reflect and Relate:

1. What is one of the tings you listed as hard to cast off?

   Why is it difficult to let go of? How might your life or relationships be different if you did cast it off?

2. What is one of the things you listed as difficult to put on?

   Why is it difficult to wear? How might your life be different if you put it on?

Prayer:

Dear Lord, we thank you today for the guiding light of your word and all of the knowledge it imparts. Lord, we sit today in need of a new wardrobe. Guide us and help us to clean our out spiritual closets, to cast off the darkness and to put on the armor of the light. Thank you for revealing these truths to us. In Jesus' name, Amen.

Prompt: For strength to break bad habits

Praise:

For Others:

For Me:

Thanksgiving:

Word Study [LIGHT]
By Jana Kennedy-Spicer

Defining "light"

light : [lahyt]

Noun
1. Something that makes things visible or affords illumination
2. An illuminating agent or source, as the sun, a lamp or a beacon
3. The radiance or illumination from a particular source
4. Mental insight; understanding

Verb
1. To set burning; kindle; ignite
2. To give light to; furnish with light or illumination
3. To cause to brighten, especially with joy
4. To guide or conduct with a light

These are just a few of the definitions for the word *light*. I always select a focus word from my scripture reading to define further, as this can really help draw out the application of the scripture. Sometimes defining the word helps to understand the word itself, but what really brings insight is to take each of these definitions and overlay them with the presence of God and really watch them unfold. As we move through our study, we will discover that the scriptures will reveal God as the source and fulfillment of each of these definitions of light.

In Other Words

In a similar manner, I also like to use a thesaurus to identify synonyms and antonyms of the focus word.

- [adjective - illuminated] bright, brilliant, cloudless, glowing, radiant, sunny, well-lit
- [noun - luminescence] beacon, blaze, bulb, candle, daybreak, daylight, gleam, glow, incandescence, lamp, lantern, lighthouse, morning, shine, splendor, sun, torch
- [verb - illuminate] brighten, flood, furnish with light, illume, radiate, light up, make visible, shine, switch on

Sometimes the best way to really understand what a word means or what it is, is to understand what it is not.

- Antonyms: dark, dim, gloomy, obscure, heavy weighted, difficult, darkness, dull, extinguish, put out, oppressive

Diving Deeper

2. Read each of the definitions of light listed on the previous page. Consider how God has acted in one of these manners as the light in your own life and write about the experience below.

Remembering how God has been present in our lives is one of the best ways to strengthen our faith that He will be present again in our time of need.

"If you say in your heart, 'These nations are greater than I. How can I dispossess them?' you shall not be afraid of them but you shall remember what the Lord your God did to Pharaoh and to all Egypt, the great trials that your eyes saw, the signs, the wonders, the mighty hand, and the outstretched arm, by which the Lord your God brought you out. So will the Lord your God do to all the peoples of whom you are afraid." Deuteronomy 7:17-19 (ESV)

2. Review the antonyms (opposite meaning) listed on the previous page. Circle any antonym which could be used to describe a current situation, circumstance, relationship or area of your life.

3. Write a prayer below, giving this area or situation to God, and asking Him to shine His presence into this area of your life, to provide illumination and understanding.

DAY 5

No Longer Formless and Empty
By Tara Blake Hatton

> "Again Jesus spoke to them, saying, 'I am the light of the world. Whoever follows me will not walk in darkness, but will have the light of life.'"
>
> John Eight : Twelve

The light of the world. The light of life. *Jesus Christ*.

The Bible is a story about light overcoming darkness, life overcoming death, love overcoming fear.

The Bible is a story about Jesus, the Son of God, who is both fully human and fully divine.

From Genesis to Revelation, the entirety of Scripture points to Jesus, *"the Alpha and the Omega, the First and the Last, the Beginning and the End."* Revelation 22:13 (ESV)

For many of us the creation story is familiar, but sometimes, when we take another look, God will reveal fresh truths to our heart. Take a few moments to revisit the creation story in Genesis 1. This story is more than the creation of the world; in it we can also see our own creation story as we are new creations in Christ.

Let's look at these two passages together:
> *"Therefore, if anyone is in Christ, the new creation has come: The old has gone, the new is here!"* 2 Corinthians 5:17 (NIV)

> *"In the beginning God created the heavens and the earth. Now the earth was formless and empty, darkness was over the surface of the deep, and the Spirit of God was hovering over the waters. And God said, "Let there be light," and there was light. God saw that the light was good, and he separated the light from the darkness."* Genesis 1:1-4 (NIV)

Just as the earth was "formless and empty" before God spoke the world into being I, too, was "formless and empty" before Jesus, "the Word made flesh" spoke into me.
> *"And the Word became flesh and dwelt among us, and we have seen his glory, glory as of the only Son from the Father, full of grace and truth."* John 1:14 (ESV)

Darkness covered the surface of my heart. I was drowning in my own sin and in the darkness of the world but, ... *the Spirit of God was hovering*.

After half a lifetime spent trying to form and fill myself, when I finally stopped striving and started to surrender, for the first time I saw myself as I truly was - formless and empty.

And when I asked Jesus to come fill me, *He did*. I was filled by Jesus, the light of life, and I became a new creation in Him. He brings us from dark to light, from death to life.

God sees the light of Jesus in us and He sees the light is good. He sees us as good, not because of anything we ever will or ever could do but because we are covered by the blood of Jesus. It is His light burning brightly within us.

Jesus says to me and to you:

> *"You are the light of the world ... Let your light shine before others,
> that they may see your good deeds and glorify your Father in heaven."* Matthew 5:14-16 (NIV)

So, as the song says, we let our little lights shine.

And then, as we shine our little lights for His glory, He continues His creative work in us. He continues to form and fill, to gather and separate. He begins to separate the light from the darkness within our souls.

He illuminates and He reveals and He uncovers hurt and pain we have long ignored and avoided. Jesus takes us by the hand and walks with us into our own broken darkness.

He walks with you, shines His light into the depths of your spirit to reveal sin and shame, pain and hurt.

But He doesn't expose the hard places only to leave you there; gaping open, bleeding and raw.

He brings your darkness out into His light so He can heal and restore and make your brokenness whole.

And *complete*. In Him.

That's Jesus. The light of the world. The light of life.

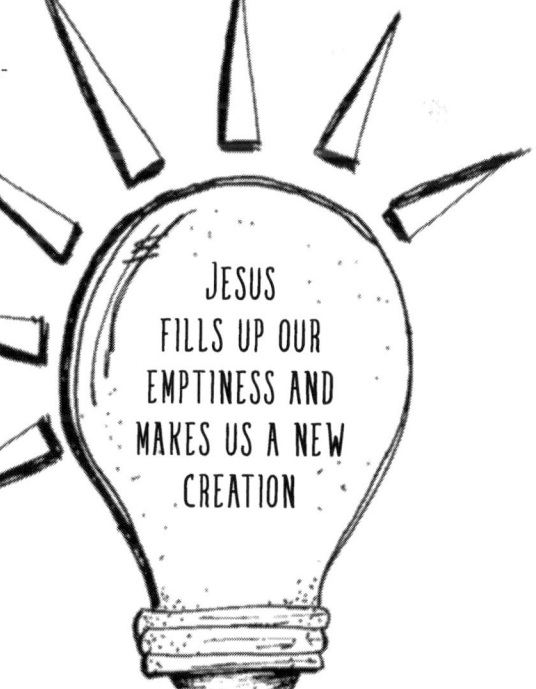

JESUS FILLS UP OUR EMPTINESS AND MAKES US A NEW CREATION

Read:

1. Read Psalm 139:13-14, did you know God knows you intimately because He created you purposefully? Yes, you were created on purpose.

   "For you created my inmost being; you knit me together in my mother's womb. I praise you because I am fearfully and wonderfully made; your works are wonderful, I know that full well." (ESV)

   How does knowing that God personally knit you together impact the way you view yourself?

Reflect and Relate:

1. Many of us take Jesus' command of "Follow me" to heart; we want to go and serve and proclaim His name. And while He does commission us to "Go and make disciples" what if his invitation to follow Him is not to go out but to go in, into the parts of our heart we have shielded and guarded?

   Is there are area of your heart you are guarding?

   How does Jesus want to grow your trust and faith in Him? In what ways does He want you to follow Him?

2. What are some ways you can let your light shine for Jesus today? In your home, in your workplace, and in your community, how can others see Jesus, the light of the world through you today?

Select one of these actions and make a commitment to shine our light for Jesus.

Prayer:

Father God, I thank you that I am your creation, your masterpiece. I thank you that I was chosen in you before the creation of the world. I thank you that you continue Your creative work in me, to form and to fill my soul, to gather and to separate the light and the darkness within me. God, I thank you that You search my heart and you know what is within better than I do. God, please continue to search me, to know me, and to show me. "Create in me a pure heart, O God, and renew a steadfast spirit within me." From the heavens to the depths, from the wings of the dawn to the far side of the sea, there is nowhere I can escape your love; you have promised to guide me, to hold me in your hand. I thank you, God, for sending Your Son Jesus who came "into the world as a light, so that no one who believes should stay in darkness." Thank you for Your great love, a love so great that you sent Your Own Son to rescue me from the darkness. And thank You for Your Word to guide me, to be "a lamp for my feet and a light for my path." God, please give me the courage to follow You into my own heart and to trust that Your work within me is good. In Jesus' name, Amen.

Prayer Journal

Prompt: Guidance to follow God's path for your life

Praise:

For Others:

For Me:

Thanksgiving:

Let Your Soul Be Inspired

DAY 6

The True Light of God
By Jennifer Cardinal

> "The sun shall be no more your light by day, nor for brightness shall the moon give you light; but the LORD will be your everlasting light, and your God will be your glory."
>
> Isaiah Sixty : Nineteen

The other day I picked up a new make up item – blush or rogue as some call it. I have not normally worn blush but as I am starting to approach the big 5-0, well let's just say, make-up is appreciated.

I opened up my new blush and swiped my blush brush across the palettes of different colors of pink that somehow magically combine to give you the perfect tone of rose for your cheeks. At first glance, I thought I looked a little odd but as I brushed out my hair and put myself together I had to admit that my face looked a bit brighter, rosier, and hey maybe even younger … (OK, maybe that's a stretch).

As I thought about what the blush did for my face, it made me think a little deeper upon the light that Christ brings to my soul.

I think we all crave sources of "light" in our lives and are drawn to things that make us maybe not only look brighter but feel brighter. In this pursuit, sometimes we look to things that are false and may temporarily provide what seems a source of light, but they don't truly sustain us. Sometimes we look to things that when the washcloth of life comes, just like the blush, they are washed away.

For me, growing up and even into adulthood, it was relationships – I had what I call Cinderella syndrome. I believed that when my prince in shining armor came, I would jump up on his white horse and he would whisk me away and all would be right with the world. At least in my world.

Well, it didn't happen that way.

In fact, I went through one broken relationship after another until I finally realized this dream was not real. *No man could save my soul.*

It was then that I was introduced to Christ, really coming to Him as a last resort. He found me, even in the midst of my darkness, and slowly as I came to know Him more and more, He healed those broken places for me.

My life did not become perfect by any stretch of the imagination but for the first time that empty place I always felt and yearned for someone to fill became filled as I spent time with Christ and poured out my prayers upon Him.

God PROVIDES TRUE LIGHT, EVEN IN THE DARKEST OF PLACES.

I came to know a light that worked from the inside out. It was a light that proved itself to not only be real but to sustain itself in my trials, my ups and downs, my doubts and questions.

God teaches us in Isiah 60:19:

> "The sun will no more be your light by day, nor will the brightness of the moon shine on you, for the LORD will be your everlasting-light, and your God will be your glory." (ESV)

We no longer need to look for sources of light from the outside as He will light us up from the inside. He alone is enough. He alone will sustain.

As He promises in Deuteronomy 31:8

> "It is the LORD who goes before you. He will be with you; he will not leave you or forsake you. Do not fear or be dismayed." (ESV)

I still put on my blush in the morning and I like the way it brightens up my face but I know that the blush will wash off. I know it's not real.

However, the sustainer of our souls lives inside us. He provides true light even in the darkest of places. We can rely on Him. He is real. He illuminates us from the inside out.

A light to which none can compare whether it be the sun by day or the moon by night or even the promise of a knight is shining armor—God alone is the one true light.

Diving Deeper

Read:

1. God teaches us in 1 Thessalonians 5:5: *"For you are all children of the light and of the day; we don't belong to darkness and night."* (NLT)

   What does it mean personally to you to belong to the light?

   How does this make you feel as you face dark circumstances or dark times in your life?

2. Jesus proclaims in John 8:12: *"Jesus spoke to the people once more and said, 'I am the light of the world. If you follow me, you won't have to walk in darkness, because you will have the light that leads to life.'"* (NLT)

   What do these words from Jesus say to you? How does this bring us freedom? How can we walk in this truth in our day to day lives?

Reflect and Relate:

1. What sources of light have you sought which have proven to be false or you now recognize to be false? How have these proven to be temporary?

2. Too often we can look to false solutions when we have a broken place which is in need of healing. Is there a broken place in your life where you can welcome God into?

Prayer:

Father God, please forgive us when we look to things of the outside world to bring us light. Father we are broken, we have dark places that are sometimes hard to reveal but we know you see it all. Father help us to bring to you our broken places. Help us know you are our safe place. Help us to trust and know that you love us. We are your children and you desire nothing more than to live inside us and bring us your true light that we may live in your glory. We surrender all this to you Lord. We trust you and we thank you for being our light and leading us to what is true, what is pure, and what will sustain us. In Jesus name we pray all this – Amen.

Prompt: For clear focus

Praise:

For Others:

For Me:

Thanksgiving:

Let Your Soul Be *Inspired*

DAY 7

Pale by Comparison
By Patti Selvey

> "By its light will the nations walk, and the kings of the earth will bring their glory into it."
>
> Revelation Twenty-one : Twenty-four

Groggily, I took my position on the hotel balcony. Pulling a sweater across my t-shirt clad shoulders, I shivered in the morning air.

The rising steam from the cup of dark roast kissed the spring morning "Hello".

"It's too early," I murmured to my 'morning person' husband. "We're on vacation."
This was more than a vacation. Celebrating our 30th anniversary, it was the first trip taken without our 5 kids. After decades of dreaming, we'd arrived in northern Arizona.

Within a few moments, rose and violet hues flashed over the Sedona Red Rocks. Blue streaks pulled through the mulberry mosaic like salt water taffy. A pensive stillness blanketed the stoic masses as the promise of a new day glimmered above.

Slowly, soft pure light began to rise above the peaks with its rays bursting forth. The pinks and purples faded into intense shades of tangerine, apricot and lemon.

The sun's beams stretched forth like a child waking in the morning after a night of rapid growth--- yawning, stretching and declaring with innocent freshness, "I'm up now. What's for breakfast?"

Soon the citrus sky yielded to vivid blues as the blazing sun shown above the jagged structures. Clouds danced in dazzling whiteness. The Red Rocks stood in majestic contrast to the abundantly deep blue sky. Ah, the glory of God's creation!

As spectacular as this sunrise was, it pales to the coming splendor of God's kingdom.

How do I know? I've read the end of the Good Book--- Revelation.
Spoiler Alert: In grand majesty, GOD WINS!

Revelation is authored by Jesus Christ. (Revelation 1:1) Jesus gave visions to John, His beloved disciple, while John was exiled on the island of Patmos. Revelation unpacks the spiritual battles waging plus prophetically outlines future events. It describes what is now unseen and what will unfold.

> ***"By its light will the nations walk, and the kings of the earth will bring their glory into it"***
> Revelation 21:24 (ESV)

There will be a New City—a New Jerusalem! Heaven will be on earth forevermore! Like the temple of the Old Testament, the New City will be God's dwelling place. The sun and moon will be unnecessary. God's great presence will provide the City's Light and Jesus, the Lamb of God, will be the lamp. (Revelation. 21:23)

"will the nations walk….."

Who are the nations? The 'nations' are the believers who persevere in Christ through trials and persecution prior to the coming New Jerusalem. Those who endure will be the City's citizens. The phrase "will walk" literally means "in the way we should live" or "behave".

"…..and the kings of the earth will bring their glory into it".

God's majesty will demand that all bow to Him. Even the most powerful rulers of the earth will bend low before the true King of Kings and Lord of Lords. They will humbly present themselves into the Light of God's presence.

There will be no more tears, illness and death. No more suffering or hardships. Sin will cease. Our enemy Satan will be completely defeated. We will dwell in the eternal state with God the Father and Jesus the Son forever in absolute peace! Maybe you are like me thinking, "Life is hard NOW. The promise of the New City feels so far away."

How can we walk in the pain of today's trials with the hope of the glory to come?

- *Live in the Light.* The Holy Spirit is with us now. At any moment, we can pray to our Father and be heard. We are never alone, never abandoned, never forsaken. The Bible is His Word to us providing wisdom and guidance. It reveals who God is and what He has done. God doesn't change! We can count on Him. Take time to pray and read His Word every day.

- *Remember whose you are.* As believers in Christ, we are dearly loved, wholly-accepted and adopted sons and daughters of the Most High. We are His. You are His! Bought with the blood of Christ and sealed in His Holy Spirit—you are marked with a promise and destined for a purpose. Claim your identity in Christ.

- *Live with the End in Mind.* Remember our spoiler alert? God wins! If you are on His team, you win, too! Whatever you are facing, it ends with God victorious if you are in Christ Jesus. We can live in the confidence that God is bigger and stronger than any situation we face. His ways are higher and His love is deeper. God is for you! And if He is for you, who can stand against you? Develop an eternal perspective.

Diving Deeper

Read:

1. Read Romans 8:18, *"For I consider that the sufferings of this present time are not worth comparing with the glory that is to be revealed to us."* (ESV)

   What are some of your present sufferings?

   How does knowing that a future glory will be revealed to us in Heaven help you to deal with situations of today?

2. Read 1 John 1:5, *"This is the message we have heard from him and proclaim to you, that God is light, and in him is no darkness at all."* (ESV)

   Recall and describe the most beautiful earthly light display you have witnessed.

   Can you imagine that this earthly beauty does not even compare to God's heavenly light?!

Reflect and Relate:

1. How can we walk in the pain of today's trials with the hope of the glory to come?
   Invite the Holy Spirit to reveal to you how you can grow in each area of your spiritual life. We can be confident God desires greater peace for us!

- Live in the Light.

- Remember whose you are.

- Live with the End in Mind.

Prayer:

Heavenly Father, You are glorious! We look forward with hope to Your coming kingdom and being in the Light of your presence. In the meantime, strengthen us in the hard places of our lives. Help us to fix our eyes upon you and the hope of the glory to come! May we stand firmly in our identity as a child of God--- never alone, never abandoned and never forsaken. We love you so much, Lord. We pray in the precious name of Jesus Christ. Amen

Prompt: For our country to follow God

Praise:

For Others:

For Me:

Thanksgiving:

Let Your Soul Be Inspired

DAY 8

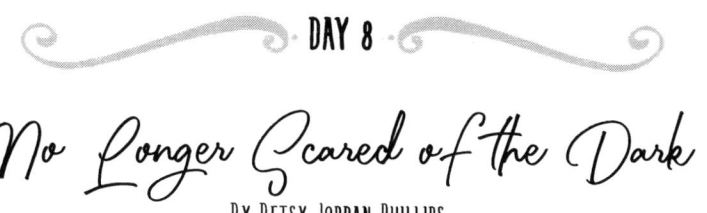
No Longer Scared of the Dark
By Betsy Jordan Phillips

> "THE UNFOLDING OF YOUR WORDS GIVES LIGHT;
> IT IMPARTS UNDERSTANDING TO THE SIMPLE."
>
> PSALM 119 : 130

Growing up, I was scared of the dark. I was that kid who always wanted a night light left on, whether in the room I shared with my sister or at least out in the hallway. Pitch black darkness just terrified me. Seriously, if the lights went out during an ice storm in Georgia, I scared the living daylights out of the rest of my family with my ear-piercing shrieks. Surrounded by darkness, I had to find someone to hold…and fast!

Maybe that's why I started playing this silly "dark" game with my children.

When they were little, just three or four years old, and would want to snuggle in my lap or curl up with me in the bed, we would face each other and draw up our hands to shield both sides of our faces. Slowly inching our faces together, our hands met and suddenly it grew dark right in front of us. Then we would whisper in our most secret voices, "It's dark in here!" Just as quickly, we would unfold our hands, letting the light stream in, finding ourselves once again safely face-to-face with the one we love.

Darkness. It can be scary. Confusing. Lonely.

We've all known darkness…literally. Haven't we all found ourselves at some point driving down a dark road, walking along a path shrouded in shadows, or plunged into "can't see our hands in front of our faces" blackness during a power outage?

We breathe a sigh of relief when we turn a corner and find the streetlights glowing.

Our rapid heart rate slows as we step out of the shadows into the moonlight.

Our loneliness and fear ease when we hear the familiar and comforting hum of the electricity returning, sure the light will follow at any moment.

Light. It casts out fear, brings understanding and helps us see we are not alone.

David knew what it was like to be surrounded by darkness, perhaps not literally but figuratively. He knew what it was to be afraid, to feel confused and to be alone.

Yet he also knew where to find the light, to seek comfort, understanding and guidance. In Psalm 119, he points us in the right direction.

There's no denying that Psalm 119 is a lengthy psalm - 176 verses, to be exact. Thank goodness it's broken up in shorter sections! It is an acrostic psalm with each of the 22 different sections beginning with a character from the Hebrew alphabet. Despite these sections, the Psalm as a whole speaks much of God revealing Himself through His Word.

Throughout the Psalm we learn that God's Word is good and true.
- His laws are trustworthy.
- His promises are sure.

In other words, *what God says is a reflection of who He is.*

⇒ When we find ourselves in darkness, whether because of our own choices or because we are suffering the consequences of choices others have made, we crave the light.
⇒ When our circumstances leave us broken and bewildered, we first ask, "Why?" We want to understand what's happening in our lives.
⇒ When we feel alone, we reach out hoping to find a hand to grasp.

So here's the thing.

The more we get to know God through His word, the brighter the light shines. The deeper we dive in to the Scriptures, the more we understand His purposes. The longer we spend unfolding the truths of what He says, the closer we feel to the Author of truth.

Just like my children and I would open our hands, dispelling the darkness and letting the light shine through, so does God's word push back the darkness in our hearts and minds. Of course, it's not just a matter of reading His word that does so, but we must also *obey* what it says.

Psalm 119 tells us over and again that God's commands, laws, statutes and precepts are to be obeyed, not just read. Each small step of obedience that we take throws back the shutters of our hardened hearts and lets the light shine in! Each simple act of trust draws us closer to our God who reveals himself throughout the Bible!

Today you might be crying out, "It's dark in here!" You might be afraid. You might feel you just don't understand what's happening in your life. You might feel alone.

Take heart. Your Heavenly Father won't leave you grasping in the dark for His hand and not reach out to hold you.

As you unfold His truth each day, you'll find light streaming through the shadows and you'll find yourself face-to-face with the God who loves you more than you could ever imagine.

> THE MORE WE GET TO KNOW GOD THROUGH HIS WORD, THE BRIGHTER THE *light shines*

Diving Deeper

Read:

1. Read Isaiah 50:10. *"Who among you fears the Lord and obeys the word of his servant? Let the one who walks in the dark, who has no light, trust in the name of the Lord and rely on their God."* (NIV)

    Walking "in darkness" suggests a lack of trust in God, a failure to depend on Him. How would trusting God shine a light on the darkness in your life today?

2. Read 2 Corinthians 3:18, *"And we all, who with unveiled faces contemplate the Lord's glory, are being transformed into his image with ever-increasing glory, which comes from the Lord, who is the Spirit."* (NIV)

    What are we told happens as we spend more and more time in God's presence?

    Have you witnessed this transformation in someone's life? In your own life?

Reflect and Relate:

1. What do you find most challenging about spending time with God in His Word?

   What changes might you need to make to overcome these challenges?

2. In 2 Corinthians 3, Paul reminds us that Moses had to wear a veil to cover the brilliance of his face after he had spent time face-to-face with God. Paul goes on to say if we meet with God ourselves, face-to-face, we won't come away unchanged! We will actually become more like Jesus!

   How do you want God to change you as you spend time in His presence and in His Word?
   List two or three attitudes or aspects of your character you can surrender to Him today.

Prayer:

Oh God, when I meet with you and read your word, don't let me come away without being changed. Open my heart and mind to the light of your truth. In Jesus' name, Amen.

Prompt: A deeper understanding of God's Word

Praise:

For Others:

For Me:

Thanksgiving:

Let Your Soul Be Inspired

DAY 9

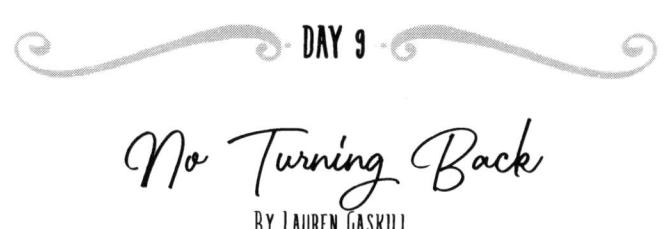

No Turning Back
By Lauren Gaskill

> "You are all children of the light and children of the day. We do not belong to the night or to the darkness."
>
> First Thessalonians five : five

Several months ago I woke up in the middle of a nightmare with a traumatic flashback fresh in my mind.

My heart was racing, my chest was tight and my body was drenched in sweat. I tried to shove the memories playing in my head to the side, but I couldn't shake the feeling of sheer panic. In my delirium I struggled to catch a breath and got up to splash some water on my face.

The cold water refreshed me as it washed away my beads of sweat, but seconds later I felt tears taking their place.

Usually I would have stopped the water works from getting too out of control. You know, stuff the tears back where they came from. But this time, as the rolled down my cheek, I didn't try to stop them. Like a rushing river I just let them flow.

I looked at myself in the mirror and scowled. What's wrong with you? Seriously ... you're pathetic. You should be ashamed of yourself right now.

I knew these thoughts were lies from the enemy, but the longer I stared at myself the more I started to consider them. Sure, there is always hope in Jesus, but part of me felt hopeless, like a Humpty-Dumpty who could never be put back together again.

Darkness has a way of making us question who we really are.

If you've seen any of the Star Wars movies, you're probably familiar with the Force. There's the Living Force (i.e. Yoda and Obi-Wan Kenobi) but there is also a Dark Side (i.e. the Sith and Darth Vader). Here's the thing: Vader didn't always belong to the Dark Side.

Like so many of us he began his journey as an innocent, wide-eyed child of the day. But somewhere along the way the darkness found him, and it made him question who he was. Suddenly he was lost and confused — fighting a battle against light and dark while forgetting his true character.

Friends, we too face a similar battle each and every day. There is an enemy. There is darkness. And it will do everything it can to blindside us and steal our joy and identity in Christ.

On the night of my flashback several months ago, I was blindsided by my past — by something I thought I'd dealt with but was resurfacing once again. The darkness found me and the enemy was trying to beat me down.

THE JESUS INSIDE OF ME IS *stronger* THAN THE DARKNESS THAT THREATENS TO OVERTAKE ME.

But I know better.

Deep in my soul I know the Jesus inside me is stronger than the darkness that threatens to overtake me.

I also know who I am.

I am a child of God. A child of the light and of the day. A child with 24/7 access to joy, love, peace, hope and the power of the Holy Spirit. A child whose Heavenly Father loves her no matter what. A child who can face the darkness because the light inside her can help her overcome anything.

You see, there is a darkness but we don't belong to it. And not only do we not belong to it, but it also has no authority over us.

Friends, I don't know what darkness you may be struggling with in this season. But whatever you're facing, I want you to know the darkness does not control or define you.

There was a time in my life where I let my struggles define me, but I'm not going back there — to the darkness, to the night, to the overwhelming pit of despair. And neither are you. Because we have been called into the light — into abundant life. And we don't have to even entertain the darkness because as children of God it's not who we are. It does not define us.

God is the only one who defines us. So let's run into the light. Run into the truth. Run to God's word. And run into His arms — where we truly belong.

Diving Deeper

Read:

1. Read Romans 8:31-39. Circle the words that speak to you the most, then go back and read it out loud.

   "What then shall we say to these things? If God is for us, who can be[a] against us? He who did not spare his own Son but gave him up for us all, how will he not also with him graciously give us all things? Who shall bring any charge against God's elect? It is God who justifies. Who is to condemn? Christ Jesus is the one who died—more than that, who was raised—who is at the right hand of God, who indeed is interceding for us.[b] Who shall separate us from the love of Christ? Shall tribulation, or distress, or persecution, or famine, or nakedness, or danger, or sword? As it is written, "For your sake we are being killed all the day long; we are regarded as sheep to be slaughtered." No, in all these things we are more than conquerors through him who loved us. For I am sure that neither death nor life, nor angels nor rulers, nor things present nor things to come, nor powers, nor height nor depth, nor anything else in all creation, will be able to separate us from the love of God in Christ Jesus our Lord. " (NLT)

   What does it mean to be more than a conqueror? How does God enable us to have this kind of strength?

2. In 2 Corinthians 5:17-18, Paul tells the church what it means to be a new creation in Christ. As you read the scripture, ask God to reveal areas of your past that you might still be holding on to. Lay them down at His feet and ask Him to help you let go.

   "Therefore, if anyone is in Christ, he is a new creation. The old has passed away; behold, the new has come. All this is from God, who through Christ reconciled us to himself and gave us the ministry of reconciliation." (ESV)

Reflect and Relate:

1. If there are areas of your past that God is asking you to lay down, write those down as an act of surrender.

2. Give those fears and scars over to the Lord and let Him remind you that you were made to walk in the light. There is no darkness, shame or condemnation — only light and glorious restoration.

Prayer:

Lord you know we long to walk in the light and to leave the darkness behind. Help us not be overcome by the night if and when it comes. Help us remember that our struggles do not define us. Help us receive our identity from you and you alone. Remind us of the promises and truths you have spoken over us, and fill us with your peace and hope right here, right now. In Jesus' Name, Amen.

Prompt: For a brother / sister in Christ in need

Praise:

For Others:

For Me:

Thanksgiving:

Let Your Soul Be Inspired

DAY 10

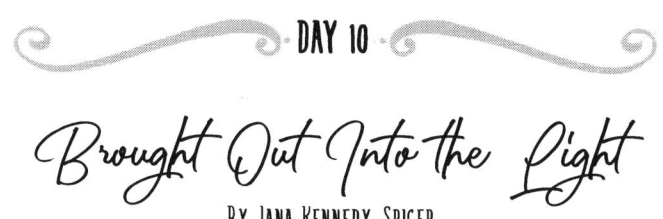

Brought Out Into the Light
By Jana Kennedy-Spicer

> "I will bear the indignation of the LORD because I have sinned against him, until he pleads my cause and executes judgment for me. He will bring me out to the light; I shall look upon his vindication."
>
> Micah Seven : Nine

I was sixteen and a senior in high school. And I knew I was in trouble. What passed as rebellion for this church girl was staying out past my curfew, and I was way past my curfew.

My mom was normally who I butted heads with in this type of situation, so as I drove home I was mentally preparing for the battle of words I knew would ensue.

When I opened the door though, I didn't see my mother. Instead, sitting on the couch impatiently waiting for his very late daughter, was my dad. Uh-oh.

He didn't say anything, just stood up. I walked over, handed him my car keys and simply uttered, "I'm sorry." Then made my way to bed.

As I lay there I felt the full weight of my father's disappointment. I was in the wrong and I knew it. I silently prepared myself to face the morning and whatever punishment would be coming my way.

In our scripture today, we find Micah poetically telling us of Zion's repentance.

Let's back up just a bit and look at the setting. In the time of Micah, God's people were divided. The twelve tribes have rebelled and battled, settling into two territories, Israel and Judah. Neither were following God. Throughout the book of Micah, the prophet tells of the sins and judgments of Israel and Judah. Today's verse picks up right when the nations become repentant and renew their faith in God.

This scenario of rebellion from God leading to sin, sinful actions leading to judgement and consequences, suffering consequences leading to repentance, repentance leading to forgiveness and restoration, and restoration leading to renewed faith and relationship with God IS the story of Israel.

And it is our story also.

I was surprised, when the morning after my late night curfew breaking, my father gave me back my car keys. *Forgiveness.* He forgave me of my transgression and restored what it had cost me. I think for the first time I truly understood what forgiveness looked – and felt – like.

The forgiveness God offers is on a scale that we really can't comprehend yet. A teenaged girl getting her car keys back doesn't even begin to compare to the glory of God's forgiveness. If you've never been on the receiving end of someone's forgiveness, it may be difficult to see God's forgiveness in the proper context. God's forgiveness is life-giving, it is transforming, it is liberating, and it brings us into the light. It is also free. Free because Jesus Christ purchased it for you, for me, for any and every one willing to accept it. God only requires one thing from us – *repentance*.

Repentance is sorrow for and hatred for one's own sin, expressed with the purpose of amendment, and comes from a love of God. True repentance is so much more than "I'm sorry."
- It is recognizing that what I did was a sin against God and being genuinely sorry – I need to repent.
- It is owning that I am a sinner and confessing my sin – I need to confess.
- It is doing what needs to be done to change my behavior and not commit this sin again – I need to change.

> *"Therefore, repent and return, so that your sins may be wiped away, in order that times of refreshing may come from the presence of the Lord."* Acts 3:19 (NASB)

The writer of Acts tells us it's not enough to just repent of our sins, we must "return" to God. We must turn in toward God instead of moving further away.

Repentance plays a vital role in our salvation. But it is not a one-time thing. Wouldn't it be wonderful if when we first come to God with our repentant hearts and receive the gift of salvation, that we would never need to repent again?

But, sadly, that's not the case. Oh, once we have received God's gift of salvation, we can never lose it.

> *"For I am sure that neither death nor life nor angels nor rulers, nor things present nor things to come, nor powers, nor height nor depth, nor anything else in all creation, will be able to separate us from the love of God in Christ Jesus our Lord."* Romans 8:38-39

We can, however – and do – continue to sin. Why? Because it is our nature inherited from Adam and his original sin.

> *"For I know that nothing good dwells in me, that is, in my flesh. For I have the desire to do what is right, but not the ability to carry it out. For I do not do the good I want, but the evil I do not want is what I keep on doing. Now if I do what I do not want, it is no longer I who do it, but sin that dwells within me."* Romans 7:18-20 (ESV)

So just like God's chosen people, the nation of Israel, we find ourselves in the same cycle of sin, consequences, repentance, forgiveness and restoration.

And just like Micah writes related to God's people, with our repentance, *"He will bring me out to the light, I shall look upon His vindication."*

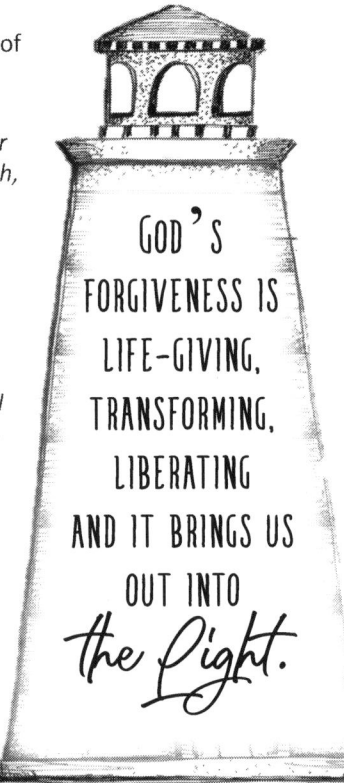

GOD'S FORGIVENESS IS LIFE-GIVING, TRANSFORMING, LIBERATING AND IT BRINGS US OUT INTO *the Light.*

Diving Deeper

Read:

1. Read 2 Chronicles 7:14. *"if my people who are called by my name humble themselves, and pray and seek my face and turn from their wicked ways, then I will hear from heaven and will forgive their sin and heal their land."* (ESV)

    What does this scripture say is required of God's people?

    What happens if we do those things?

2. Read 2 Peter 3:9. Circle the words that describe God. *"The Lord is not slow to fulfill his promise as some count slowness, but is patient toward you, not wishing that any should perish, but that all should reach repentance."* (ESV)

    Why does God want us to repent?

Reflect and Relate:

1. Do you have any unconfessed sin in your life? Take this time to confess and repent, asking God for forgiveness.

2. Are there any changes you might need to make in your life to break any habits of sin?

Prayer:

Father God, we thank you for your patience, for your long-suffering, for your desire to bring us to repentance and the gift of our grace and forgiveness. We are not worthy of this blessing. Forgive us for the sin in our life we hold on to, and equip us to break the cycle and habits of sin in our lives. Thank you for hearing our prayers and healing our hearts. In Jesus' precious name, Amen.

Prompt: For God to reveal anything in your life not pleasing to HIm

Praise:

For Others:

For Me:

Thanksgiving:

Let Your Soul Be *Inspired*

DAY 11

Be Careful Little Eyes What You See
By Missy Millspaugh

> "THE EYE IS THE LAMP OF THE BODY. SO, IF YOUR EYE IS HEALTHY, YOUR WHOLE BODY WILL BE FULL OF LIGHT."
>
> MATTHEW SIX : TWENTY-TWO

I remember it as if it were only a few weeks ago and not fifteen years.

At the time, my children were eight and nearly three years old. So, you can imagine there wasn't a lot of news being watched in our home in the mornings. This was also well before Amber Alerts and push notifications on your phone. This was back, when you really only used your cell phone for emergencies and texting was way too expensive for normal people.

So, I was devastated and totally in shock when I got into the car to take my daughter to school and heard what was happening in New York City on the radio. It was, as we were driving to the school, that the second plane hit the South Tower.

My heart was broken.

Once I finally returned home, my mother-in-law had the news on. It was then that I saw not one, but two buildings topple to the ground. I saw people running through the streets of Manhattan, scared, injured, and confused. I watched as they told of another plane crashing into the Pentagon and yet another crashed into a field taking the lives of all the passengers, but sparing the intended target.

I watched and watched and watched.

The more I watched, the more my heart broke. Here I was, 1200 miles away, but I felt like it was happening to me, in my city, to my family and friends. But, I continued to watch. I watched all day, I watched for several days.

That was the problem.

It's funny that what we see can have an effect on how we feel, what we think about, what we do.

When we look at things that are distressing, even if it isn't happening to us, we feel distressed. How about when we see silly cat videos, children playing, or sadly, pornographic images as we flip through the channels on our television. How do they make us feel? Do we linger? Did we stay glued to the set? We watch something on T.V., at the time thinking it's no big deal, only to dwell on it later? It becomes all we think about, even when we are no longer watching. Those Hallmark commercials would not hit so close to the heart if they were only sound.

Our eyes are the window to our whole body, what we see has a lasting effect.

This is why we protect our eyes when we are about to see something scary, we close our eyes when we are going around the loop on a rollercoaster, we shield our child's eyes when there is something inappropriate.

There is a saying, *'you can't un-see that'*; and it is true. Our brain is like a camera and our eyes are the lens. Once we see it, our brain has taken a picture and stored it in our memory. The longer we look; the more pictures are saved. When we recall those dark, unwanted pictures, they bring darkness, but when we recall those pictures that are fun, full of love and life, there is glorious light. Like a great day at the beach.

I didn't want to leave my house, I didn't want my daughter to go to school, I didn't want my husband to go to work; I didn't want to run the risk of something happening to any of us. I thought, '*I live in the fourth largest city in the US, they could be targeting here.*' I thought we would be safe, if we were at home.

After about three days of watching the aftermath of the attack on 9/11, I realized that I could no longer watch the news; it was stealing my joy, my hope. I realized that if I didn't start focusing on something that would give me peace, that I would continue to spiral downward. I had to come to the realization that God was in control, that no matter what happens, He is still taking care of me. He is still protecting my family. But, **I had to get my focus off of what was bringing me down and turn my focus to what would lift me up.**

OUR EYES ARE THE WINDOW TO OUR WHOLE BODY, WHAT WE SEE HAS A LASTING EFFECT.

I remember the first time I had to drive somewhere that was outside of my neighborhood. I had to drive to the other side of town and it would require me to drive right through the middle of downtown. It was a beautiful day, cloudless blue skies; the kind of day people write about. The only difference was there were not a lot of cars on the road in our busy city and there were still no airplanes in that beautiful blue sky.

As I drove through town that day, I cried. I cried for those who lost their lives, I cried for the families that would no longer be able to see the ones they loved. I cried for a people who didn't know those people but felt so passionate about their cause that they could take lives. And I cried for that beautiful day. Because as I drove through my city, with its tall buildings and blue skies, I saw **hope**. *And that, was really nice to look at.*

Diving Deeper

Read:

1. Read Philippians 4:8. *"Finally, brothers and sisters, whatever is true, whatever is noble, whatever is right, whatever is pure, whatever is lovely, whatever is admirable—if anything is excellent or praiseworthy—think about such things."* (NIV)

    Think about these words, write down any emotions you feel associated with these words.

2. Read Ephesians 1:15-23. *"For this reason, ever since I heard about your faith in the Lord Jesus and your love for all God's people, I have not stopped giving thanks for you, remembering you in my prayers. I keep asking that the God of our Lord Jesus Christ, the glorious Father, may give you the Spirit[f] of wisdom and revelation, so that you may know him better. I pray that the eyes of your heart may be enlightened in order that you may know the hope to which he has called you, the riches of his glorious inheritance in his holy people, and his incomparably great power for us who believe. That power is the same as the mighty strength he exerted when he raised Christ from the dead and seated him at his right hand in the heavenly realms, far above all rule and authority, power and dominion, and every name that is invoked, not only in the present age but also in the one to come. And God placed all things under his feet and appointed him to be head over everything for the church, which is his body, the fullness of him who fills everything in every way."* (NIV)

    Paul refers to the 'eyes of your heart;' they allow you to see as God's sees. What are some areas in your life that you need to see how God sees?

Reflect and Relate:

1. Think of a time that you saw something you couldn't 'un-see.' How did it make you feel?

2. Now write down a time you saw something that made you feel whole, at peace, joyful.

Prayer:

Precious Heavenly Father, we love you. We ask you to help us see with new eyes; eyes that see as You see. Help us to determine if what we are looking at is lifting us up or bringing us down. Remind us that when we put our focus on you, we don't have to worry about the darkness, because you are the Light of the World. Thank you for Your Holy Spirit who gives us a little nudge when our eyes are drifting. In Jesus name, Amen.

Prompt: To see yourself as God does

Praise:

For Others:

For Me:

Thanksgiving:

Let Your Soul Be *Inspired*

DAY 12

Finding Redemption in the Light
By Gretchen Fleming

> "FOR IT IS YOU WHO LIGHT MY LAMP, THE LORD MY GOD LIGHTENS MY DARKNESS."
>
> PSALM EIGHTEEN : TWENTY-EIGHT

David knew the depth of dark times- when life becomes unrecognizable and confusing from what was once the norm, or expected. He had been a shepherd boy minding his own business in the fields of his father, as he watched over the flock entrusted to his care. He was comfortable where he was. Then God came calling through the prophet Samuel, anointing him to be the next king of Israel.

David heeded the call and left the security of his "norm" as he stepped out in faith. He was a shepherd boy chosen to be king, quite a lofty expectation from someone so young and inexperienced. But he obeyed nevertheless, trusting the God who watched over him in the fields to care for him in the palace. Only the path to the palace was not what he could have predicted.

David did what he thought was right by God and his countrymen, as he accepted this new call upon his future, but what he received in return was confusion, betrayal and uncertainty.

In other words... darkness.

The Hebrew word David used in Psalm 18:28 for darkness means *obscurity, ignorance and misery*.

As he faithfully served the current King Saul and nation of Israel, he faced giants in battle along with raiding enemy armies. Waiting on God's timing for his ascension to the throne, he sought to love God and others as he attended King Saul, while also fighting fearlessly in the military. David exemplified selfless service. But as his successes increased, so did his enemies.

What became so confusing for David were the accusations and betrayal of his own countrymen. From King Saul, whom he loyally and sincerely served, to his own friends, David felt betrayed.

David responded like he had learned to do in the fields as he encountered predators after his flock; he called upon the Lord his God. Psalm 18 describes how David cried out for help from God, seeking His intervention, His deliverance. As a shepherd himself, he had begun to see God as his own shepherd, watching out for his well-being. Therefore, it was second-nature for him to call upon the Lord personally and passionately.

And what were his expectations of the Lord? ***David knew it was God who could keep his lamp burning, sustaining him in difficult times, helping him bear up under adversity.***

When life defied logic and expectations, it was God who could still guide the way. What seemed like darkness for David was crystal clear for God, who is able to turn our darkness into light for His good purpose.
- He redeems.
- He rescues.
- He transforms not only our circumstances, but us as well.

And as David was refined by his tumultuous path to the throne of Israel, he was good and ready for what the Lord required of him- to shepherd God's kingdom to the honor and glory of His Name!

Sometimes, life just doesn't make sense. We don't understand why it has to be so hard or arduous. As a logical person, I really struggled with this during a time in our family's life where the path to the future took an unexpected turn for the worse.

What I thought was waiting for my son as he left home to begin his career was anything but rosy and wonderful. As someone who had struggled most of his life with learning issues, he had experienced more than his fair share of trials. So when he had graduated from technical school and moved to another city to work, I thought "Finally! Now we can relax and have it easier ." I hoped he could begin a new chapter by experiencing success instead of struggles, happiness instead of hardships.

Well, it went horribly wrong from our expectations and like David, I felt confused and uncertain. I remember being at work after hearing from my son that he had lost the job he loved so much. He was devastated......and so was I.

In that moment, I turned to the Lord, crying out for help. I needed guidance and clarity when all seemed to be illogical and dark. God sustained us through His strength as we experienced those dark days. It was God who held us, who carried us when we had no ability to continue on. He "lightened our darkness" little by little, and what once was hopeless, is now a reality.

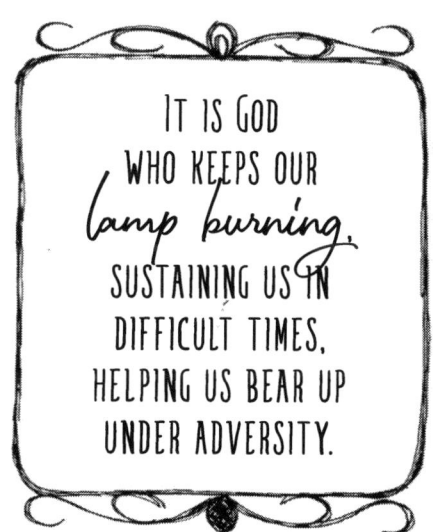

Just as David was finally delivered, so was our son as he became employed in a job he loves and is now enjoying success. It took years, and did not make sense at times, but like David, we called and God responded, keeping us going until our darkness was lifted. The obscurity of our path was enlightened, and the misery redeemed, while we were refined more like our Savior.

We learned that dark times happen and life does not always make sense. But when we look to God to light our way, He is there to sustain and provide, redeeming our darkness with His marvelous light.

Diving Deeper

Read:

1. Read Psalm 18:32. *"It is God who arms me with strength and makes my way perfect."* (NIV)

    David recognized that God was his source of strength. When faced with day to day struggles, do you tend to rely more on your own strength or Gods strength?

    What can you learn from David and his habits that can help you better rely on God as your source of strength?

2. Read Psalm 119:105. *"Your word is a lamp to my feet and a light for my path."* (ESV)

    For what role in his life does David give credit to the scriptures?

    What role in your life do the scriptures play? Would you say they play
    - ◊ a prominent role,
    - ◊ a secondary role,
    - ◊ an occasional role or
    - ◊ maybe even little to no role at all?

    We are all growing in Christ, we will be our entire life. What is one thing that you can do to give the Word of God a more important role in your life?

Reflect and Relate:

1. It's said we are either in the midst of a storm, just leaving a storm, or about to enter a storm. This could be a difficult time, a dark time or maybe a confusing time. David found himself confused because he was doing what God told him to do, but it seemed to have negative personal implications. God used this time to refine David, to prepare him for the next leg of his journey.

    Has there ever been a time when you looked back and realized that a previous storm was actually preparing you for a current situation? What did you learn?

2. Are you currently in a time of confusion? Has life veered from your expectations? What can be learned from David on how best to respond during these times?

Prayer:

O Lord, may we learn from David how to persevere when life gets obscure and difficult. May your Word give guidance and perspective, turning our darkness into light. In Jesus' name, Amen.

Prompt: To see your situation more clearly

Praise:

For Others:

For Me:

Thanksgiving:

Let Your Soul Be Inspired

DAY 13

God's Redeeming Grace Makes the Difference
By Mitzi Neely

> "Arise, shine, for your light has come, and the glory of the Lord rises upon you."
>
> Isaiah sixty : one

I could never put my finger on how it happened. Even today I can't explain the feelings of doom and gloom that swept over me that summer, 17 years ago.

But it happened. I can still pinpoint the feelings--the sadness, the overwhelm, the tired, and at times, the depression. I was in a dark place and I was there alone.

I did the best I could to hide it and relied solely on myself to work my way through it. After all, this kind of thing doesn't happen to someone who is always in control, always on top of a schedule, and always seeing to others.

I remember not wanting to start school that fall. I kept toying with the idea that I could resign my teaching position and be a stay-at-home mom. That was not what my husband wanted to hear, and truth be told, it sounded nothing like me.

In my mind though, I was walking around in complete darkness. I wanted to sleep all of the time, I didn't have any energy, and I didn't want to be responsible--for anything. That's pretty tough to do when you're a wife, a mom to a young teenage daughter, working a full-time job, and committed to a number of extra activities. And my poor husband--he just kept asking why, and what would I do if I walked away from my mission field.

I didn't have an answer for him. I just kept trying to rationalize and justify my thought process. Clearly this was about me and no one else.

I felt the darkness had invaded my body, much like it had enveloped the people in Isaiah 59. I felt isolated from God and with that kind of twisted thinking I may have even convinced myself that I wasn't worthy of His love and forgiveness.

God knew I was battling the evil one.

While I was doing everything I could to hold my ground and withstand his attacks on me, my faulty thinking and shortcomings were sinking me further and further into depths of despair and poor decision making. As I tried to look ahead, I couldn't see anything getting better. I had turned to reading secular articles and books, trying to find a solution to snap me out of my downward spiral, and to my dismay they didn't provide the permanent relief I was so desperately seeking.

Thankfully God intervened and sent an angel to my classroom doorstep that September day.

I believe she was working on His behalf to draw me out of the darkness and into the light.

She was the mother of one of my students, as well as a colleague. I must have been in a pretty low place to have poured out my heart to her that afternoon; but everything inside of me spilled out, and I couldn't stop.

When I finally did finish laying out the entire story of what I was experiencing, she lovingly came at me with scripture. Verse after verse and example after example of God's love for me. She shared what happens when we let darkness take root in our hearts and minds, and then she prayed for me, and over me.

She didn't stop there.

The next morning she showed up at my classroom door and gave me a couple of devotions to read from one of her favorite books, '*Streams in the Desert*,' by Charles Cowman. She had selected them specifically for what I was going through. For the first time in a long time I felt there was hope and a future.

After months of being immersed in a thick and desperate darkness, my Redeemer was providing a
glorious rescue. The Light had indeed come, but it was through His timing and His control. And when the light comes, God tells His people to respond to it, and to Arise and Shine!

The angel God sent that day was not there as an overnight miracle, but instead as a support system to walk with me through that journey. Escaping the darkness was my assignment. And as a Daughter of the King I had been equipped with the tools and resources to do just that.

Oh, how blessed I am that He called me out of the darkness of despair and defeat and covered me in His light and His glory. Oh, how His redeeming grace for a wretch like me made the difference.

Scripture is: VERSE AFTER VERSE AND EXAMPLE AFTER EXAMPLE OF GOD'S LOVE FOR ME.

Diving Deeper

Read:

1. Read Colossians 1:13. *"For He has rescued us from the dominion of darkness and brought us into the kingdom of the Son He loves."* (NIV)

   In Colossians, Paul says that true believers have been transferred from darkness to light, from slavery to freedom, from guilt to forgiveness, and from the power of Satan to the power of God.

   Describe a time in your life when you walked away from darkness and despair, and made the decision to walk in His Light as the rightful King?

2. Read Psalm 34:18: *"The Lord is near to the brokenhearted and saves the crushed in spirit."* (NIV)

   We often wish we could escape troubles that wear us down. But God promises to be 'close to the brokenhearted,' and to be our source of courage, strength, and wisdom. When trouble strikes, don't get discouraged or frustrated, instead go to the Lord in prayer and ask for His help.

   Has there ever been a time when you subconsciously allowed Satan to pollute your thinking and lead you down a path of mistruths and deception? How did you regain your footing and see God's light?

Reflect and Relate:

1. When you find yourself believing the lies of the evil one, what are some ways to help you distinguish between truth and lies and help you find your stronghold in Jesus Christ?

2. Often times when sadness or depression takes root in our mind and soul, Satan exploits this as a weakness and takes our focus off Christ. How does the prince of darkness convince us our circumstances are hopeless?

3. As children of light, our actions should reflect our faith. How can we guard our hearts from being pulled into situations that sabotage our beliefs and convince us that we are less than children of a Mighty King?

Prayer:

Almighty God, thank you for your promises and truths. Thank you for protecting us from the powers of this dark world and surrounding us with your abundant love and light. May we see your hand of grace and mercy upon us as we face trying times. Help us to walk in your ways, and to cherish all you promise to be for us in Jesus. In Your precious name, Amen.

Prompt: to step out in faith

Praise:

For Others:

For Me:

Thanksgiving:

Let Your Soul be Inspired

DAY 14

Made to be a light
By Anne B Say

> "For so the Lord has commanded us, saying, 'I have made you a light for the Gentiles, that you may bring salvation to the ends of the earth.'"
>
> Acts thirteen : forty-seven

At first glance this verse is lovely. Who wouldn't want to be a light? Who wouldn't want to take the love of Jesus to the ends of the earth? It inspires a big "yes" in my spirit and soul. And it should! Our spirits were created to say "yes" to this.

When we dig deeper into the verse we discover from the context that Paul and Barnabas are in Antioch of Pisidia on their first missionary journey. They were most likely sent there after visiting Cyprus. When they arrived Paul was invited to speak in the temple. The message was full of wisdom and insight. The message tied their religious history with the redemptive relationship in Christ. The congregation and Jewish rabbis were moved. They were asked to return the following week. The King James version records that "almost the whole city" came out that second week. Can you imagine the power and love in their message that the whole city would show up?

There are 3 responses to the situation in this story.

- *First, the God-fearing leaders and many in the town came to faith in Jesus.* They heard the message and received its gift. They rejoiced in the Messiah and were filled with the Holy Spirit. This was the plan. The results were similar to their earlier visit to Cyprus. Many believed. The text also tells us the message was spreading throughout the whole region.

- *Second, the Jewish leaders saw the crowd that showed up for the good news and took offense.* They incited the influential men and women against Paul and Barnabas. They felt threatened and humiliated that their guests had won over the people of their city. They wanted these two men gone.

- *Third, Paul, Barnabas, and those traveling with them shook the dust off their feet and left for Iconium.* They were not rejected, offended, or fearful. The text tells us they were filled with joy and filled with the Holy Spirit.

The Jewish leaders had missed it. They had missed the One they were waiting for because they had lost sight of who they were. They were God's chosen people, the light through whom salvation would come. (Isaiah 49:6) It had come, and the message was presented again, and they still missed it.

They missed it because they didn't understand how to be a light.

We are the light when we share the good news of Christ.

Paul knew his calling. He knew what he was called to do, and he did it. As he traveled, he always went to the temple and shared, then he went to the Gentiles and shared. Paul took advantage of every circumstance and situation in which he found himself. He shared the good news of Christ with each person who crossed his path.

We are the light when we know our identity and work together.

2000 years ago the people in our text struggled with comparisons. Fast forward to today with social media and 900 television channels showing us how we can decorate our homes, live our lives, and take our careers to the moon and back without breaking a sweat.

Comparisons never end well. They are indicators that we've confused our identity. Comparisons prevent us from being a light.

God has called us each to a purpose. He prepared specific works for us to do. It is through our unique purposes that we are a light to the world, that we bring salvation to the ends of the earth. We are all created with a unique design and purpose. The fullness of who we are, our quirkiness, our passions, skills, even our experiences are all designed to equip us to do the work that our heavenly Father has called us to do. Ephesians 2:10 explains that those works were planned for each of us before we were born. We are called to be a light through who we are and how we use our uniqueness to share the good news. Our skills put us in places where Jesus needs us to be a light. Our experiences help us relate to people who need an encounter with Jesus. Everything can be used by Him to bring salvation.

We are a light when we choose God's power through Holy Spirit in us.

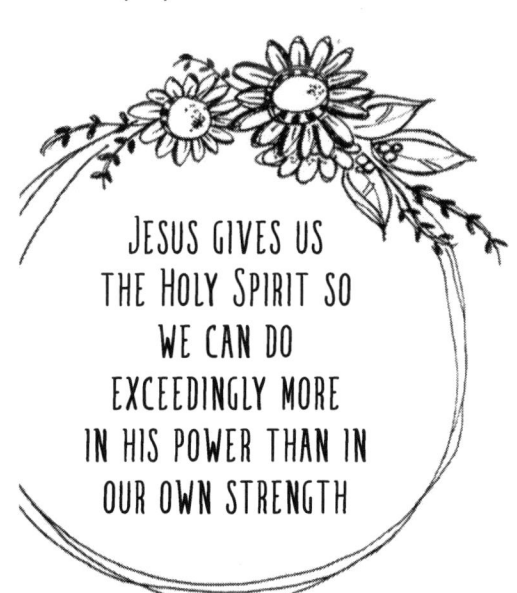

JESUS GIVES US THE HOLY SPIRIT SO WE CAN DO EXCEEDINGLY MORE IN HIS POWER THAN IN OUR OWN STRENGTH

The Jewish leaders in our story became offended at the city-wide turnout to Paul and Barnabas. They were operating in their own strength. Paul and Barnabas were operating in God's power and many came to salvation.

Jesus gives us the Holy Spirit so that we can do exceedingly more in His power than we can in our own strength. The reason everyone showed up the second week was because they were looking for some good news. The reason everyone was filled with joy is because they were filled with the Holy Spirit. The Jewish leaders in that city couldn't bring that because they didn't have it to bring.

Diving Deeper

Read:

1. Read Psalm 139:13-18.

   *"For you formed my inward parts; you knitted me together in my mother's womb.
   I praise you, for I am fearfully and wonderfully made. Wonderful are your works; my soul knows it very well. My frame was not hidden from you, when I was being made in secret, intricately woven in the depths of the earth. Your eyes saw my unformed substance; in your book were written, every one of them, the days that were formed for me, when as yet there was none of them. How precious to me are your thoughts, O God! How vast is the sum of them! If I would count them, they are more than the sand. I awake, and I am still with you."* (ESV)

   List the words and phrases which describe how you were made:

2. Read Luke 9:12-17.

   "Now the day began to wear away, and the twelve came and said to him, "Send the crowd away to go into the surrounding villages and countryside to find lodging and get provisions, for we are here in a desolate place." But he said to them, "You give them something to eat." They said, "We have no more than five loaves and two fish—unless we are to go and buy food for all these people." For there were about five thousand men. And he said to his disciples, "Have them sit down in groups of about fifty each." And they did so, and had them all sit down. And taking the five loaves and the two fish, he looked up to heaven and said a blessing over them. Then he broke the loaves and gave them to the disciples to set before the crowd. And they all ate and were satisfied. And what was left over was picked up, twelve baskets of broken pieces." (ESV)

   The Lord is able to use everything in our lives, no matter how small and insignificant. What might you bring Him to be used as a light in your corner of the world?

Reflect and Relate:

1. Consider all of who you are. God created your wonderful self. Jesus died for all of your wonderfulness. If there is an area that you see as less than wonderful, ask Him to redeem it. Ask Him to use it as a light for others.

2. Think about your skills, passions, and hobbies. How could God use you to build relationships with others so that you can be a light in their lives?

Prayer:

Dear Jesus, Help me to understand and embrace how wonderfully you made me. Help me to see how to use my skills, passions, and experiences to be a light for you, to bring salvation into my corner of the world. Help me to love you more by loving myself and others as you do. In Christ's name, Amen.

Prayer Journal

Prompt: To be aware of your divine appointments

Praise:

For Others:

For Me:

Thanksgiving:

Let Your Soul Be *Inspired*

Bible Study *Tools*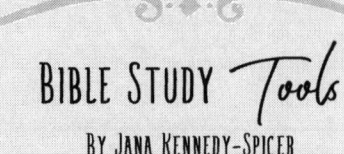

By Jana Kennedy-Spicer

Wouldn't it be wonderful if we could just open up the Bible, begin to read and receive divinely inspired understanding? Well, God does communicate with us through the scriptures, and we are told if we lack wisdom, just to ask and God will supply our needs.

But if we're being real, most of the time, it just doesn't happen that way. We have a hunger, a desire to read and study and learn the Bible, but we sit looking at the cover not knowing—and sometimes a little nervous about—where to start. I've been there, actually find myself there often. If you do too, don't worry, there are a lot of Bible Study resources available.

So I would like to share some information about some of the Bible Study Tools I have found helpful in my journey to dive soul deep in to God's Word.

- **Bible Reading Plans:** An organized listing of scripture references designed to help guide a reader through the Bible.

⇒ Just opening the Bible and starting to read doesn't work very well. And because the Bible is actually a collection of books, letters and poems written by multiple authors in a variety of styles, it doesn't read like a regular book. Meaning you don't just begin reading on page one and read through to the end. You see, the Bible isn't written in order. Even in a single book, written by a single author, the writings may not be in chronological order.

⇒ So, a reading plan is a great place to begin. There are many, many Bible Reading Plans. Some, like our devotional, are topical, others are chronological, or even book by book.

- **Bible Dictionary:** A great resource to help define and analyze scripture. Provides a combination of definitions and proper names for Biblical words. A Bible Dictionary allows the user to define words and study them in context relative to the proper theological concepts of the specific verse. Many word searches also include the original Greek and Hebrew words with meaning.

⇒ When studying the Bible it's very important that we understand the truth in the meanings and lessons intended at the time of the writings. We can then take those lessons and ask God how it can impact our lives today. A Bible Dictionary helps us to answer the question, "what does that word really mean?"

- **Parallel Bible:** Compares multiple translations of the Bible side by side. It can help you see how different translations interpreted the original language.

- **Bible Commentary**: Typically written by theologians and offers explanations and interpretations of the scriptures. They can offer great insights and background information about the authors, history, setting and context. Verse by verse teachings can be found by many great Christian leaders.

⇒ Use commentaries to draw out a deeper meaning of scripture. It is important, when studying the Bible, to apply the proper teachings and not overlay our own meanings or understandings.

⇒ Commentaries offer unique and exclusive access to the minds of great theologians. We can learn directly from them and no longer have to 'wonder' what something means.

- **Concordance:** An alphabetical listing of words present in a text, in this application, specifically the Bible.

⇒ At the back of your Bible is an 'abbreviated' concordance, which contains only some of the words in the Bible. An 'exhaustive' concordance is a book all on it's own, and contains all of the words in the Bible, even the 'and' and 'the', etc.

⇒ Use the concordance to look up a specific topic or word. You will find a list of scripture references where that word is used. This is a great resource to find multiple scriptures relating to a specific topic or word, like our study on light.

Amassing all of these resources for yourself might be expensive, but you can also locate them at most libraries. If your church has a library, check there first.

However, I use all of these resources on-line. There are many websites and even apps which can be downloaded to your phone and tablets. Here are a few of my favorites:

- **BibleHub.com**

Some of their resources include: the Apocrypha, an Atlas, over 25 Bible translations, almost 30 Commentaries, a Concordance, Devotions, Dictionary, Encyclopedia, Greek and Hebrew texts, a Library, Multilingual Bibles, Photos, Reading Plans, Sermons, a Study Bible. Biblical Timeline and a Topical Bible.

BibleHub.com in a free on-line resource which also offers a free downloadable device app.

- **BibleStudyTools.com**

Some of their resources include: several Bible translations, audio books, reading plans, Parallel Bible, Interlinear Bible, topical listing, Apocrypha, library, devotionals, videos, Commentaries, Concordances, Dictionaries, Encyclopedias, Lexicons, Bible Trivia, Sermons and Sermon illustrations.

- **Bible.org**

Study the Bible by book, topic, author or verse. Also find resources specifically tailored to men, women or children.

These are just a few of the many, many on-line free resources available and designed to aid in the study of God's Word. I encourage you to try them out, see what feels comfortable to you. But also make sure that whatever resources you use are grounded in solid Biblical truth.

DAY 15

Seen by God
By Terry Holmes

> "But when anything is exposed by light, it becomes visible"
>
> Isaiah nine : two

When I think about this verse it's easy to picture a flashlight shining into the darkness. Do you remember those scenes out of the scary movies when they're opening a closed door and all you can see after it's open is wherever the flashlight is pointing to?

Just like that flashlight, God is light. It's part of who He is. When I think about this quality to Him where His light can "expose" anything, it all sounds kind of scary too. It's like being on the movie screen and the flashlight is showing Him inside of me. It feels far too close.

At first, I didn't know if I liked that he saw so much of me because that would include everything - all of my flaws, every thought and even every unmet dream. But at the same time, I can't take this trait away from Him. I can't change who God is or what He sees. It's just part of Him being God...and I'm glad for it. His light isn't just to see inside me, it's the lens he views all people and every situation under heaven through.

**There came a time when I finally wasn't afraid
that God knew everything and saw everything because it meant he was for me.**

I once had a conversation with someone at a business. I was given the total price of an item but my credit card statement showed an entirely different amount being charged. When I called the store about the discrepancy, I was told the price that had been quoted was only an estimate. Except, I never heard the word "estimate"; it was presented as the full price. Suddenly the phone was being handed from one person to the next and I was asked to explain what had happened over and over again. By the end of the phone call, I was told to accept what was charged or cancel the order. The whole experience left me feeling frustrated because even though I knew what I had been told about the item, no one else did.

Have you ever experienced feeling misunderstood? Have you ever been in a situation where it felt like no one else was for you or you were being unfairly mistreated?

As frustrated as I was by what happened, God's response to me was, *"So have no fear of them, for nothing is covered that will not be revealed, or hidden that will not be known"* Matthew 10:26 (ESV).

He already knew all the pieces to this entire experience. He knew all the words of each person, the heart motivations of each person, even the background that each person operates from giving Him the full landscape over every piece in its entirety. Every. Piece.

HIS CHARACTER OF BEING LIGHT IS WHAT REVEALS THOSE PIECES BECAUSE HE ALONE IS THE TRUTH.

God was showing me that in the end, it didn't matter who was right or who was wrong. Those pieces were for God to carry; all that mattered was that He saw me. He wasn't using His "light" against me or to hurt me. He was using it to comfort and assure me.

I love that God isn't like a person. I love that His heart is to care for us and comfort us, rather than looking to point out when things are wrong. He cares about these seemingly small moments in our life and is by our side even when it feels like no one else is. Knowing this about Him is what helps me trust Him.

You can be sure that that if He cares enough about that small conversation, He also cares about the bigger things happening in our lives too.

We can trust Him when He says He will never leave us or forsake us in Hebrews 13:5-6.

> "God has said,
> 'Never will I leave you;
> never will I forsake you.'
> So we say with confidence,
> 'The Lord is my helper; I will not be afraid.
> What can mere mortals do to me?'"
> (NIV)

Beloved daughter, let us take comfort in His light.

Diving Deeper

Read:

1. Read Psalm 139:1-4. Notate the words or phrases which tell us what God knows about us.

    "You have searched me, Lord, and you know me. You know when I sit and when I rise; you perceive my thoughts from afar. You discern my going out and my lying down; you are familiar with all my ways." (NIV)

    Does understanding that God knows all of these things about you bring comfort? Why or why not?

    Are there things in your life you have tried to hide from God?

2. If you continue reading in chapter 139 of Psalm, verse 5 tells us *"You have enclosed me behind and before, And laid Your hand upon me."* (NASB)

    How does the truth of verse 5 impact your comfort or concern that God sees and knows everything about you?

    Can you recall a time when God intervened on your behalf because He could see what was ahead for you, but you could not?

Reflect and Relate:

1. Has there ever been a time when you felt misunderstood?

   How does it change that experience to know that His light reveals all things?

2. Do you believe God is for you?

   If not, what keeps you from knowing that?

Prayer:

Lord, I thank You that You know everything. I thank You that Your light assures us of how You are for us even when unfair or tough times happen. Please help us to always see You as someone who is for us. In Christ's name, Amen.

Prompt: To better understand someone else's position

Praise:

For Others:

For Me:

Thanksgiving:

Let Your Soul be Inspired

DAY 16

Flip on the Light Switch
By Jodie Barrett

> "Light is sown for the righteous,
> and joy for the upright in heart."
>
> Psalm ninety-seven : eleven

Walking into dark houses with no power can be frightening! But I've walked in them over and over.

My family looks at houses for a living. Every day we walk up to houses that we know are empty and knock on doors. After no answer, we unlock the door, and poke our heads into the unfamiliar spaces and announce our presence just in case someone happens to be in the darkness.

Admittedly, I do fine if light is streaming in the windows to showcase the cracks and crevices of the unfamiliar. But there are those houses with blinds or curtains over every glass pane that block the light. Those leave me frightened until my eyes adjust!

Walking through life can be like walking into unknown, dark houses with curtains over the windows.

Have you ever been there? Have you ever stood in unfamiliar places that bring on fear?

Behind every door we walk up to there can be something good or bad. You may not be walking up to houses like my family. But there are other doors we each encounter and have the choice to open.

The door of a new job.

The door of a new school.

The door of starting a new family.

The door of moving to a new town.

The door of _____ (insert what door you are approaching).

I don't know about you, but I like to be able to flip a light switch on when I enter the dark. Here is the good news. There is a light switch for every area of life we enter! It's not found on the wall of a house, but it can be carried with us so that every time we walk forward we can know that light will be scattered into the unknown. This light comes from knowing Jesus.

Psalm 97:11 (NASB) says, *"Light is sown like seed for the righteous and gladness for the upright in heart."*

I like to say it this way,
"light is planted all around those who know Jesus and joy is ready for them".

When we share a relationship with Jesus He is at work for us! Jesus becomes the planter of light in an otherwise dark world.

Picture little candles being lit in a dark room; at first the small flames look dim compared to the darkness. Then, as your eyes adjust you can see even into the smallest cracks. The light scatters across the unknown spaces!

After getting married my husband and I moved to a new city. It was large and unknown. The whole town looked unfamiliar and every door we opened was new. We needed a new home, we needed jobs, we needed friends, and we needed a place to worship. My husband had to leave our home for an extended time to train for his job. I was left to face every new door alone. I had the choice of living in fear or in trusting Jesus to light the way. I admit there were times I walked up to a door, knocked, and ran, forgetting that I was not alone.

Have you ever needed a flashlight and couldn't find one? Or you found it and the batteries were out?

That was where I found myself. Things felt dark and I couldn't find a flashlight that worked. Looking back I know that I was trying to turn on switches with no power. I wasn't spending time in prayer or in my Bible. Those two things help us know Jesus better. Prayer and Bible study can flip a light switch on in a dark room.

Jesus is the light switch for those who believe!

Jesus always has power!

"You, LORD, keep my lamp burning; my God turns my darkness into light." Psalm 18:28 (NIV)

The next time you are entering a dark house, a new space in your life, remind yourself that you carry within you a light switch. To turn on the power, you simply believe and call His name, Jesus.

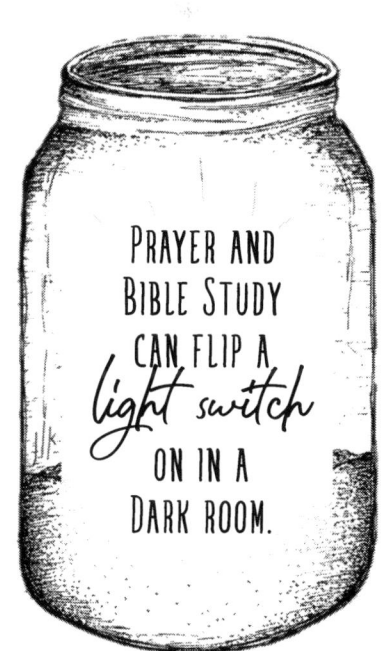

Diving Deeper

Read:

1. Read 2 Timothy 1:7. Circle what God gives to us.

   "For God hath not given us the spirit of fear; but of power, and of love, and of a sound mind." (KJV)

   When facing circumstances which include a factor of the unknown, are you typically fearful or confident? Indicate on the scale below where you typically find yourself.

   Fear | | | | | | | | | Strong

   What factors contribute to your fear or your strength?

2. In Deuteronomy 31:8, we are told *"It is the LORD who goes before you. He will be with you; he will not leave you or forsake you. Do not fear or be dismayed."* (ESV)

   How does the truth of this verse impact your fear factors?

   What truth in this verse gives you strength?

Reflect and Relate:

1. Can you recall a time that you were afraid to walk forward into something new? Maybe you were even being pushed forward.

   After reading today's lesson, how could you now react differently?

2. Has there ever been a time that you ran away from something unknown because you felt alone and unsure?

   How can today's scriptures bring you confidence the next time you face the unknown?

Prayer:

Father, The world can look dark and frightening when we face the unknown. Help us to trust that you are the power that scatters light into every crack and crevice. Help us face new doors without fear. As we trust you and call your name, light the way! In Christ's name, Amen.

Prompt: For an opportunity to bring joy to someone else

Praise:

For Others:

For Me:

Thanksgiving:

Let Your Soul be Inspired

DAY 17

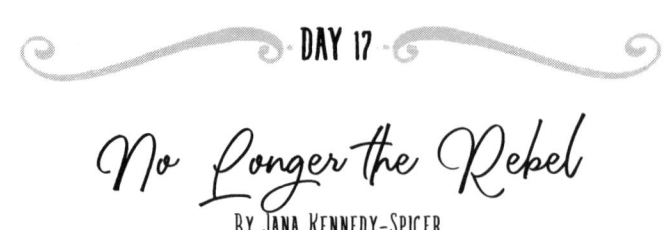

No Longer the Rebel
By Jana Kennedy-Spicer

> "There are those who rebel against the light, who are not acquainted with its ways, and do not stay in its paths."
>
> Job twenty-four : thirteen

As kids, my brother and I used to run the streets with the neighborhood kids. We didn't stay in the house unless we had to; we lived and played outside all day until the porch lights were turned on in the evening – our signal it was time to go home.

Then, every night at 10:00pm, as the news was coming on, the announcer would say, "It's ten o-clock, do you know where your children are?"

This was because "nothing good happens after dark" or "if you're out after dark, you're up to no good." I can still hear my mom's voice of warning, and even recall repeating the same sentiments to my own kids a time or two.

Simple statements, yet so full of truth and wisdom. And why is that?

Darkness (of night) offers a great place to hide, to disguise the truth, to misguide the eyes. By contrast, light (of day) reveals the truth, it makes things visible, it brings attention to actions.

Under the cover of darkness, people do things they would never do in the light of day.

In our verse today, we again meet up with Job, and he is speaking of people who do evil things at night under the cloak of darkness. He even lists some examples of their actions, in the verses following. But these are just a few of the things people do as they "rebel against the light."

Rebel. Our English dictionaries define a rebel as someone who resists authority, control or tradition; but the Greek meaning is much stronger, using words like bold and audacious when describing someone's acts of rebellion or disobedience.

Whichever definition you want to use, one thing is very clear with both: *being a rebel is a choice.*

Today's pop-culture has made being a rebel a popular label. And in some situations, the rebel has even been the one standing up for what is right. But neither of these scenarios are the type of rebels Job is speaking of.

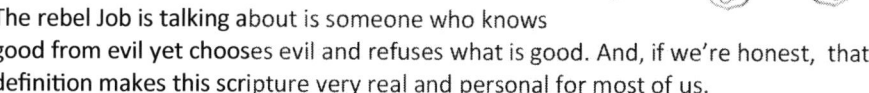

The rebel Job is talking about is someone who knows good from evil yet chooses evil and refuses what is good. And, if we're honest, that definition makes this scripture very real and personal for most of us.

Maybe you haven't done any of the things Job mentioned in verses 14-17, but
- Have you ever known the right thing to do but chose not to do it?
    ⇒ Like received too much in change and instead of returning it, chose to keep it.
- Have you ever known what God said you were to do but chose not to do it?
    ⇒ Like been in a situation where you had the perfect verbal comeback, knew you shouldn't say it but chose to say it.
- Have you known the Bible teaches not to do that thing but you chose to do it?
    ⇒ Like knowing you shouldn't gossip but that little tid-bit you just found out is just too juicy not to share, so you choose to tell it.

I could go on with examples but since I can answer "yes" to each one, I will just stop with these.

Whether you and I do or don't look the part of what society labels a rebel is not important, because being a rebel isn't about public perception, or society even. Rebelling against God is personal, it is a matter of the heart. It's about making choices every day, all day, to think, say and do things which are good and holy – *of the light* – not things which are evil and sinful – *of the darkness*. (ref Ephesians 4:17-32)

So why does someone – *why do we* – rebel against the light? Job offers two reasons:
- Not being acquainted with the light
- Not staying on the path of the light

Being acquainted with The Light

> "Again Jesus spoke to them, saying, 'I am the light of the world. Whoever follows me will not walk in the darkness, but will have the light of life.'" John 8:12 (ESV)

To be acquainted with the light we must first know who is the light. We must get to know Jesus. We must get to know God's Word. This isn't simply knowing right from wrong. We can know moral principles without knowing God.

This is about being so close in relationship with God that we know Him personally, we know His voice above all others, we know His words over the words of false teachers. The only way we can know for sure if that voice we are hearing is false or if those words we are reading are false – *is to know the truth*.

Prayer and Bible study are the best way to know God and to know His words. Then we can then spot what is not of God, we can separate what is false from what is true.

We easily recognize the voices of our loved ones, even in a crowd or without physically seeing them because we are familiar with their voice. We are constantly, daily hearing their voice. So if we want to be able to recognize God's voice above all of the others, we must also be in constant communication with Him.

Staying on The Path

> *"Trust in the Lord with all your heart and do not lean on your own understanding. In all your ways acknowledge Him and He will make straight your path."* Proverbs 3:5-6 (ESV)

How many times have you worried over a situation because you didn't' know what decision to make or which way to go? Me? Too often to count. And in my claim of not hearing from God, I typically go ahead and step out on my own, blazing my own trail.

Sounds a little like being a rebel.

In Proverbs 3:6, we see that the key, or requirement, for God defining or straightening our paths (making them know to us) is "acknowledging" Him. Other translations put it this way: submit to Him, seek His will, know Him, and consider Him.

That sounds like the opposite of rebelling.

Making The Choice

So my friends, we have a choice.

Job tells us that there are those who rebel against the light and do not walk in its path.

But John also tells us that there are those who walk in the light:
> *"But if we walk in the light, as He is the light, we have fellowship with one another, and the blood of Jesus His son, cleanses us from all sin."* 1 John 1:7 (ESV)

It's your choice. It's my choice. Walk in darkness or walk in the light?

Which do you choose?

> TO BE ACQUAINTED WITH
> *the light*
> WE MUST FIRST
> KNOW WHO IS THE LIGHT.
>
> WE MUST
> GET TO KNOW JESUS.
> WE MUST
> GET TO KNOW GOD'S WORD.

Read:

1. Read Ephesians 4:17-24. *"Now this I say and testify in the Lord, that you must no longer walk as the Gentiles do, in the futility of their minds. They are darkened in their understanding, alienated from the life of God because of the ignorance that is in them, due to their hardness of heart. They have become callous and have given themselves up to sensuality, greedy to practice every kind of impurity. But that is not the way you learned Christ!— assuming that you have heard about him and were taught in him, as the truth is in Jesus, to put off your old self, which belongs to your former manner of life and is corrupt through deceitful desires, and to be renewed in the spirit of your minds, and to put on the new self, created after the likeness of God in true righteousness and holiness."* (ESV)

   Fill in the words or phrases which are used to describe the Gentiles?

   - _____ in understanding
   - _____ from life
   - _____ in them
   - _____ of heart
   - Become _____
   - Given to _____
   - Greedy to practice _____

2. Continue reading, Ephesians 4:25-32, Circle the things we are to put off, or do away with.

   "Therefore, having put away falsehood, let each one of you speak the truth with his neighbor, for we are members one of another. Be angry and do not sin; do not let the sun go down on your anger, and give no opportunity to the devil. Let the thief no longer steal, but rather let him labor, doing honest work with his own hands, so that he may have something to share with anyone in need. Let no corrupting talk come out of your mouths, but only such as is good for building up, as fits the occasion, that it may give grace to those who hear. And do not grieve the Holy Spirit of God, by whom you were sealed for the day of redemption. Let all bitterness and wrath and anger and clamor and slander be put away from you, along with all malice. Be kind to one another, tenderhearted, forgiving one another, as God in Christ forgave you." (ESV)

   For each item circled, list below what that action should be replaced with.

Reflect and Relate:

1. Are there any areas of your life where you are actively rebelling from God? Large or small, list one or two of them below.

2. What habits, ways of thinking, or attitudes in your life might need to be "put off" so that you can "put on" the new self, created after the likeness of God in true righteousness and holiness?

   Put Off Old Self   Put On New Self

Prayer:

Dear Lord, we thank you for your guiding light and the redemption and healing you bring to our sinful lives. Forgive our moments of rebellion, big and small, any rebellion from you is sinful. Oh redeem us and make straight our paths. Show us Lord, the rebellious attitudes in our hearts, reveal to us any area of our lives, actions, thoughts, and words which need to be put off so we can put on the beautiful new life you give. Thank you Lord for answering our prayer. In Jesus' name, Amen.

Prompt: For God to expose where I have veered off the correct path

Praise:

For Others:

For Me:

Thanksgiving:

Let Your Soul be Inspired

DAY 18

By Mitzi Neely

> "Come, O house of Jacob, let us walk in the light of the Lord."
>
> Isaiah two : five

When my daughter was little, she was afraid of the dark. Night after night I went through the motions of getting her ready for bed, prayed with her, and then tucked her into bed. Thinking we were all set for hours of deep slumber, the calm would last little more than five or ten minutes before I heard, 'Mama. Mama, come here.'

There was always something for me to check out. Look under the bed she would say. Open the closet door so she could take one last look around. Leave the door cracked so she would know we were close by.

This mama sometimes felt her patience wearing thin. My ability to take care of daily chores and prepare for the next day was getting some serious interference from the calls in the darkness.

Each time I was summoned to her room for one last 'look-see,' I knew what she really wanted was to prolong the inevitable--bedtime. It was the 'being alone' part, coupled with the dark of night that got her.

It didn't matter how many times her dad and I reassured her, she just wanted there to be light.

And when you think about it, don't we all? In a dark place don't we long to see a light shine?

One of my favorite quotes by Andy Andrews says, "If darkness is winning the battles, my friend, it is because the light is not doing its job."[1]

After many attempts of getting her to settle in for the night, we finally were able to comfort her with a night light and a 'Psalty' Singing Songbook[2] tape. What we considered to be small and insignificant, made all the difference.

The night light provided just the right amount of illumination in her room so that she could distinguish between shadows and objects, reassuring her she was safe. And Psalty's singing character provided extra reassurance through scripture, hymns, and storytelling.

In the midst of her fear, a touch of light and a bible-believing children's character gave her God's word to store in her heart.

I'm not sure bedtime would have gone very well if we hadn't had these resources to lead her out of the darkness and into the light. But they did just that.

I am reminded of my precious girl and her nighttime shenanigans as I studied the passage in Isaiah where God calls His people to transform their thinking, reorient their worldview, change their behavior, and come into the light.

Much of the darkness we encounter in our lives exists in our heads. Just as it had for a little girl fearful of what the darkness would bring at bedtime.

It was more about concentrating on the negative aspect, when we should have been concentrating on walking in the light of God's word.

Allowing the darkness to invade our thoughts essentially sends us into a downward spiral of negativity. What God wants is for us to cast a bright light through our positive attitude of gratitude.

DARKNESS HATES THE LIGHT OF GRATITUDE. BUT OH HOW OUR FATHER LOVES THE LIGHT!

So you see the choice is ours. We can continue to go our own self-absorbed way and dwell in the depths of darkness, or we can choose to glorify God and follow His instructions. It is a matter of choosing to remove ourselves from a dark situation and move toward the light.

As we navigate our day-to-day situations we can continue to encourage others to stave off darkness as they seek God first, follow His ways, and enjoy His kingdom. And by doing this, we can truly be a light for the world.

---

[1] *The Noticer Returns: Sometimes You Find Perspective and Sometimes Perspective Finds You* by Andy Andrews; Thomas Nelson;
[2] Created by Ernie and Debbie Kerner Rettino; Kids Praise 1980; Maranatha Music; [3] lyrics by Avis Burgeson Christiansen and a tune written by composer and teacher Harry Dixon Loes

Diving Deeper

Read:

1. Read John 8:12. *"Then Jesus again spoke to them, saying, "I am the Light of the world; he who follows Me will not walk in the darkness, but will have the Light of life." (NIV)*

    Jesus brings God's presence, protection, and guidance. Describe how Jesus is the light of your world?

    How has Jesus illuminated your path as you journeyed through fear and uncertainty?

2. In Psalm 119:105 we see that in order to move safely from place to place we need a light so we won't trip over obstacles in our way. In this life, we walk through a dark forest of evil.

    "Your word is lamp to my feet and a light for my path." Psalm 119:105 (NIV)

    How does the Bible provide us the necessary light to steer clear of the roadblocks and stay on the right path?

    How has scripture given you the support and guidance you needed as you made big decisions?

Reflect and Relate:

1. When you find yourself wallowing in negativity what are some ways you can choose to step away from the darkness?

2. As you press into Him, ask God to reveal fears that keep you from being all He wants you to be.

Prayer:

Dear Heavenly Father, thank you that despite our fears and inadequacies, you love us unconditionally. As we fend off fear and the darkness that surrounds us, let us dwell in the light of your word so that it illuminates the path you have set before us. Thank you for your hand of protection as we press forward to glorify your name. In Jesus name, Amen.

Prayer Journal

Prompt: To deepen your relationship with God

Praise:

For Others:

For Me:

Thanksgiving:

DAY 19

Wondering Through the Darkness
By Adrienne Terrebonne

> "THIS IS THE MESSAGE WE HAVE HEARD FROM HIM AND PROCLAIM TO YOU, THAT GOD IS LIGHT, AND IN HIM IS NO DARKNESS AT ALL."
>
> FIRST JOHN ONE : FIVE

Shortly after our third child was born, we received military orders to move to a new state. It was a heartbreaking move for us because we had been deeply attached to the church and friends we were leaving.

Making the move even more difficult was the fact that our precious new baby was not a good nurser, and she never slept. Never. I was exhausted and lonely.

When we finally arrived in our new town, I felt very isolated. Our two-year old son was exhibiting classic signs of autism while our newborn was colicky. For thirteen months.

I couldn't leave the house without help from my husband or our oldest daughter because I couldn't manage these two difficult babies by myself. The result of this isolation was that I didn't have any friends and sadly, I lived for the days when our son's therapist would come into our home just so I could have some adult interaction.

Hello. My name is Pitiful.

Days would pass where I didn't want to get out of bed. My husband would come home from work, I would hand off the screaming baby to him and then lay down in sheer exhaustion. But sleep wouldn't come, only tears.

And all too soon, he would bring the baby back to me because he couldn't soothe her. Honestly, no one could.

It was the most awful year of my life.

I didn't want to pray.
I didn't want to see anyone.
I didn't know what I wanted.

I felt darkness all around my soul but I knew that it wasn't from the Lord. He was not the author of the depression enveloping me because his character cannot contain darkness.

Our key verse from 1 John tells us that God is light. And because his character
is light, there can be no darkness or decay in him. He is pure and holy, without defect. God is perfect. And he loves us, even though we are broken, defective and imperfect.

As I wrestled with feelings of despair and isolation, I began to dive into the scriptures. God reminded me that he has been faithful to me in the past. We need to remember this truth when we are wandering through the darkness. He has already performed many miracles in our lives.

We need to remember God's *faithfulness* when we are wondering through the darkness.

Sometimes the Lord will lead us through our own personal wilderness to test us and prove our character. Will we follow Him? Will we obey? Or will we give up when life gets hard?

Let's make the decision to get up. To take one day at a time. To pray. A lot. And to trust the Holy Spirit to provide us with the stamina and energy and faith to make it through.

I didn't suddenly snap out of my depression one day. It was a slow process of learning to trust Christ with my erratic emotions and my depressed feelings. But as I searched for him, I felt his light shine on me. He brought me out of the shadows and into his light.

And do you know what I experienced? God's faithfulness. He loves each of us so much and He wants to see us thriving in Him.

Christ is the ultimate healer. He brings light, not darkness, to our souls. He is mighty to save, friends. Pour your heart out to Him. Trust Him to lead you in the appropriate direction.

He wants you to be healed and whole.

Read:

1. Read Psalm 77:11-12. *"I will remember the deeds of the Lord; yes, I will remember your miracles of long ago. I will meditate on all your works and consider all your mighty deeds."* (NIV)

   Can you recall a time of God's faithfulness in your life?

   Why is it often difficult to see God working in tough times?

2. Read 1 Peter 1:13-16. *"Therefore, with minds that are alert and fully sober, set your hope on the grace to be brought to you when Jesus Christ is revealed at his coming. As obedient children, do not conform to the evil desires you had when you lived in ignorance. But just as he who called you is holy, so be holy in all you do; for it is written: "Be holy because I am holy."* (NIV)

   According to 1 Peter 1:13-16, how does having Christ's light in us affect our behavior?

Reflect and Relate:

1. Taking time each day to remember God's faithfulness can help us endure the times darkness seems to overtake us. Writing down these memories can provide us with a physical resource to re-read during difficult times.

    Do you currently journal?

    If so, how has this helped you deal with day to day circumstances?

    If not, how do you think incorporating this practice into your day could be a benefit?

2. Are there lingering hurts in your life? God's light of healing often requires our willingness to lay down what we are holding on to. What might you need to lay down to let in God's healing light?

Prayer:

Father, we thank you for your light when our world feels dark. Help us to seek after you. Remind us of the many miracles you have performed in our lives already and help us to be faithful in following where you lead. We love you and we want to strive to pursuing you in holiness. In Jesus name, Amen.

Prompt: Tell someone something you have learned from God

Praise:

For Others:

For Me:

Thanksgiving:

Let Your Soul be *Inspired*

DAY 20

Finding Perspective in God's Light
By Gretchen Fleming

> "FOR WITH YOU IS THE FOUNTAIN OF LIFE;
> IN YOUR LIGHT DO WE SEE LIGHT."
>
> PSALM THIRTY-SIX : NINE

I remember sitting on my yellow couch that morning already worn out by the day. I felt like I was on a roller coaster, taking twists and turns and drops out of nowhere. Only it wasn't the physical roller coaster that thrills, it was an emotional roller coaster.

It seemed like I found myself in this state of mind increasingly more often and I was just getting exhausted by it all. Why is life so dramatic? There had to be a better way. And that's when my mind automatically turned to the Bible.

One of the most life-changing lessons God has taught me has to do with perspective. Specifically, His perspective being more advantageous than mine. As I have lived life with it's ups and downs, and as my faith has matured, I have learned to quickly transition from what I am thinking about a particular situation to asking what God has to think about it.

I have found His perspective is really all that matters because of numerous reasons.

1. *God is All-Knowing* therefore He has the wisest, truest perspective that I can trust. My perspective can be skewed because of ignorance, emotions and pride.

2. *God is All-Loving* so I can trust that His perspective will always have my best interest at heart. He loves me like no other AND He loves others just as much. It is a perfect love which drives out all fear as I rest in the fact that His perspective will be fair to all in any given situation.

3. *God is All-Powerful*, bringing everything and everyone under His authority and submission. He is fully able to control and navigate me and my circumstances.

As I sat on my couch that morning, with my inadequate perspective in need of the Lord's, I understood full well that He IS the fountain of life and in Him I see things as I should. This change in perspective happens as I begin to consider what the Word has to say about my circumstance, because it is in the Bible that I learn what His perspective IS on any given situation.

For instance, that particular day I was drained from the emotional highs and lows of family life. When you have family members going through the peaks and valleys of their own lives, it is hard to not get caught up in their drama. Whether they are experiencing the greatest of achievements or the worst of defeats, it can all get to be too much. I liken it to getting caught up in their dust storm. It is way too easy to get carried away.

The tension exists as I yearn for steadiness and consistency. Mind you I am not saying flat emotions, just steady emotions. And that is what brought Jesus to my mind that day. While experiencing the ebb and flow of two family members' emotions, connected to their ongoing goals and struggles in life, I realized there had to be a better way of handling this thing called "life"!

My mind remembered Jesus in Luke 4:14-30. Jesus went from being praised in one place to being driven out of town in another. The highs of people thinking He was wonderful and then the lows of people trying to throw Him off a cliff were extreme to say the least. Yet Jesus handled it with such peace and perspective. He did not get caught up in the fame, nor the infamy. It simply said He "went on His way".

He had stayed firmly rooted in His God-given purpose, preaching the good news, knowing that the praise and persecution were under God's control and not for Him to be overly concerned with. He entrusted it to whom it was meant and then He rested in that knowledge. Jesus abided in the All-Sufficiency of His Father, which enabled Him to maintain composure.

Pondering how Jesus handled His life so calmly helped me see how I could as well. This lesson from Jesus reminds me of why I look to Him for perspective.

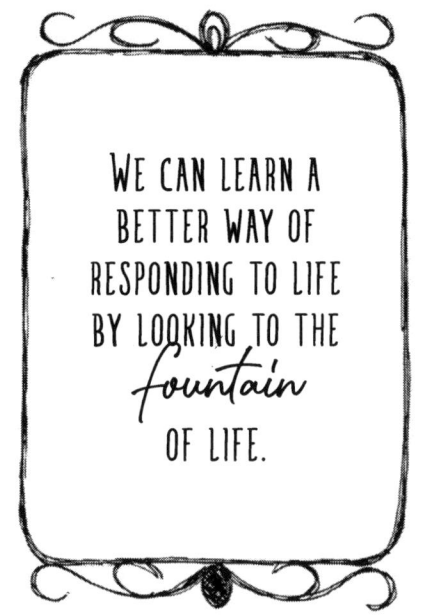

Psalm 36:9 says,
*"For with you is the fountain of life,
in your light do we see light."* (ESV)

I learned the better way of responding to life by looking to the fountain of all life and learning from His example. It was in His "light" that I saw my light, a better perspective. Who better to glean perspective from than Him?

Having lived long enough and hard enough to understand my own deficiencies, I am assured that God absolutely has the perspective I need and can't live without!

Diving Deeper

Read:

1. Read Ezekiel 12:2. circle the words that influence a person's perspective. Underline what interferes with correct perspective .

   "Son of man, you dwell in the midst of a rebellious house, who have eyes to see, but see not, who have ears to hear, but hear not, for they are a rebellious house." (ESV)

   How would being rebellious influence a person's perspective?

2. Read 1 Peter 2:9 and circle the words that describe your identification as a believer.

   "But you are a chosen people, a royal priesthood, a holy nation, a people belonging to God, that you may declare the praises of him who called you out of darkness and into his wonderful light." (NIV)

   Describe the responsibility of our identification, the response God wants from us?

Reflect and Relate:

1. What can you learn from God's Word to gain perspective on circumstances that are causing emotional upheaval in your life?

2. Ask God to reveal any rebellion interfering with your perspective on a particular matter. Identify and confess it in agreement with Him, asking for forgiveness.

Prayer:

Heavenly Father, give us eyes that see and ears that hear. May our hearts not be rebellious, clouding our way and making life more difficult. For with You we find our fountain of life, giving all that we need to find the better way through the highs and lows of everyday living. In Jesus' name, Amen.

Prompt: To find simple ways to better enjoy life

Praise:

For Others:

For Me:

Thanksgiving:

Verse Mapping
By Jana Kennedy-Spicer

If you cringed at the site or sound of "verse-mapping" or was suddenly transported back to the nail-biting days of high school English, you are not alone. I did too when I was first introduced to the study method. But don't worry. I very quickly fell in love with verse mapping, and I have a feeling you will as well.

First, know that there is NOT a wrong way to do this. The purpose of the exercise is to wring every little bit of meaning and application out of a scripture. Picture that wet towel being folded over and twisted tight to release all of the water being held. Twisted and wrung until the very last drop has been extracted.

Second, while the writing portion of verse mapping is focused on a single, or small selection of scripture, know that the study process goes well beyond a single scripture reference.

To begin, use the following blank page, or the corresponding Verse Mapping page in our Soul Deep Scripture Journal, or just grab a blank piece of notebook paper & draw a rectangle on the page. Then...

- **Select** the scripture verse to map.
- **Read the verse**.
- **Write out the verse**. (in the box, leave plenty of space around it, between the lines and between the words.)
- **Personalize it**: replace words like "you", "we", "us", "them" with your name, where applicable
- **Mark, circle, underline, highlight words and phrases that stand out to you**.
    - Any words make you want to dig deeper? Look up and define any words that need clarification.
    - Any promises from or actions of God?
    - Any action encouraged or required on your part?
- **Read the verse in context**: read the preceding and following verses or whole chapter. See how it ties in to the verses before and after it.
- **Read the verse in other translations**: note which words or phrases help you understand or apply the verse.
- **Cross-reference the verse**: find, list and read other verses which speak about the same topic.

Let the richness of God's Word flow into your soul.

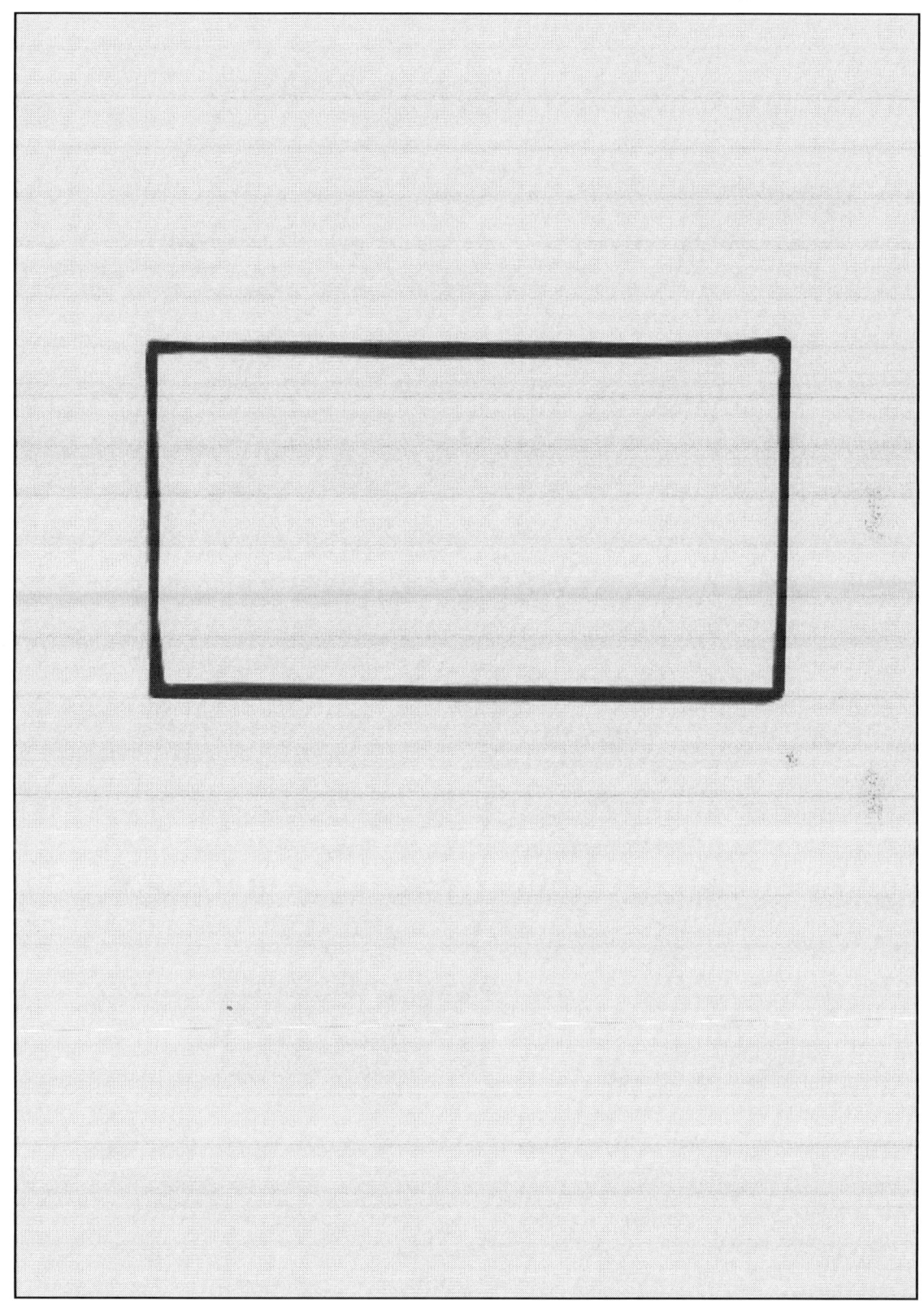

Verse Mapping Example

Write out the verse →

REVELATION 22:5

- no more darkness in heaven
  - literally – Rev 21:23 } God's glory
    Rev 21:11 } illuminates
  - figuratively – Rev 21:27 nothing evil, impure or unclean
    Rev 21:4 no mourning, death, pain, crying
    Rev 22:3 nothing accursed, unholy

Key — Who are "they"?

- Rev 22:3 His servants
- Rev 7:15 bond servants to the throne
- Rev 7:13 cleansed by the blood of Jesus
- the saved by CHRIST!

> And the (night) will be no more
> they will need no light or sun,
> for the Lord God will be their light
> & they will reign forever & ever.

→ Rev 21:23 glory of God gives light

- (Daniel 7:18,27) saints receive the kingdom — all dominions will serve the saints
- (Rom 5:17) eternal life in heaven — Received through Christ Jesus
- (2 Tim 2:12) endure persecution — Reign with God (Rev 20:4) in heaven

Cross-reference the verse

Mark, circle, underline, highlight words and phrases

Remember, there is NOT a wrong way to do this. The purpose of the exercise is to dig deeper into God's Word so we can understand it's meaning and the lesson God has waiting for us on every page of Scripture.

Verse Mapping Example

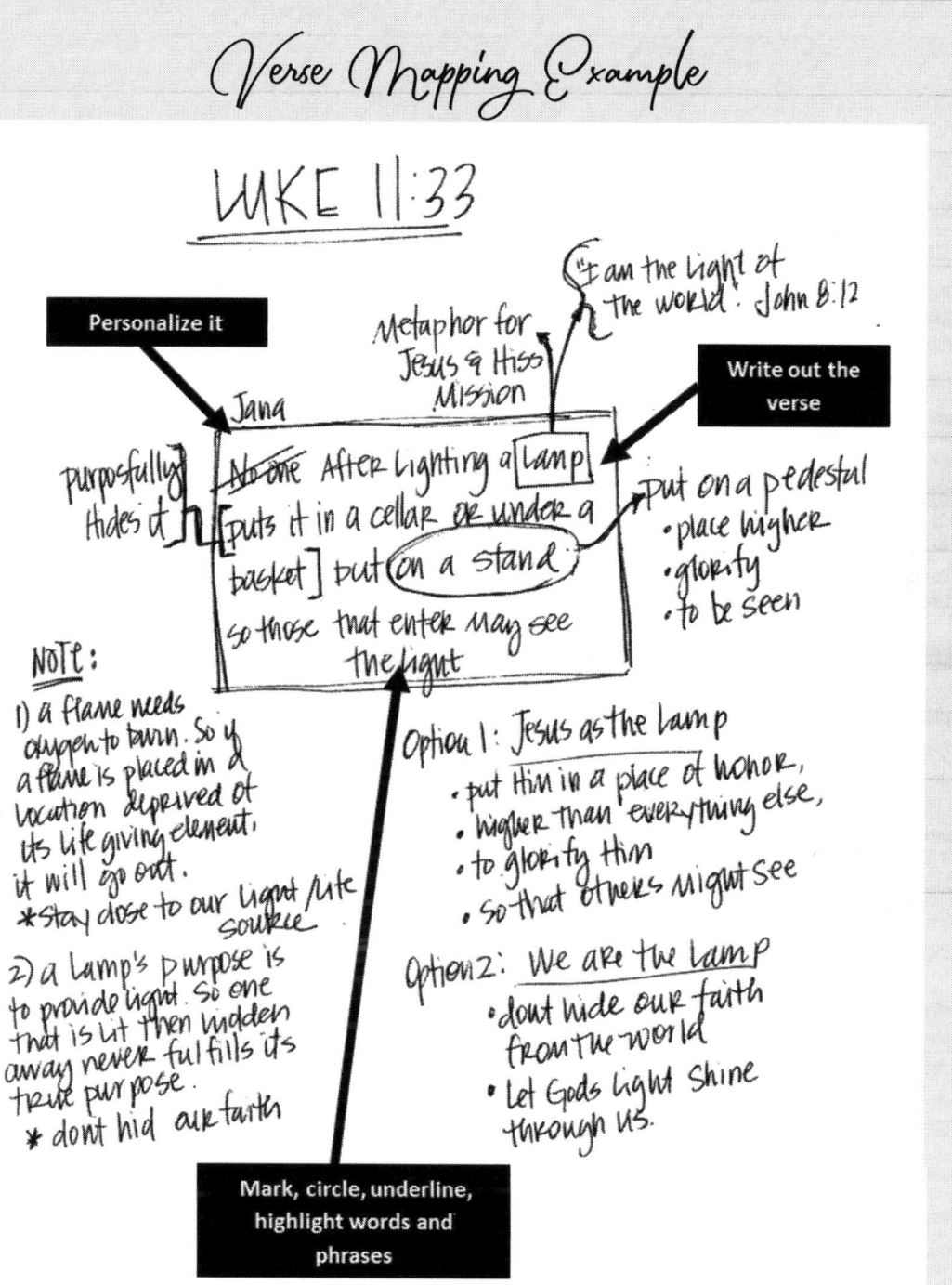

Don't be afraid to ask yourself, "what does this mean?", and then go researching. Use Bible Study Tools to help you dig deeper. Set aside anything you already know about the verse, look for the information and explanations that you don't know.

DAY 21

By Tara Blake Hatton

> "For God, who said, 'Let light shine out of darkness,' has shone in our hearts to give the light of the knowledge of the glory of God in the face of Jesus Christ."
>
> Second Corinthians four : six

Do you ever have to spend time wrestling with a verse before it starts to become clear? Sometimes it's helpful to look at a verse in smaller pieces so that God can bring the big picture together in our hearts and minds.

God said: *"Let light shine out of darkness."* At the creation of the world, God spoke light into being. He made light to shine when previously there was nothing but darkness. God does the same in each of our hearts as we are made new creations in Him. Before Jesus we were all living in the darkness of the world.

When we receive Jesus His light shines in our hearts and we begin to be transformed into His image as we are made pure and holy. (2 Corinthians 3:18, 1 Corinthians 1:30)

The final portion of our key verse, overflowing with prepositional phrases, reads: *"the light of the knowledge of the glory of God in the face of Jesus Christ."* This means that, as believers, we know that it is God's glory shining in and through Jesus; that Jesus is God Incarnate, God in the flesh.

We believe the words of John 1:14 to be true: *"And the Word became flesh and dwelt among us, and we have seen his glory, glory as of the only Son from the Father, full of grace and truth."* (ESV)

> To a believer, Jesus is the Word made flesh. (John 1:14)
> Jesus is the way, the truth, and the life. (John 14:6)
> Jesus is the light of the world. (John 8:12)

But, to a nonbeliever, many of the truths that we know and hold dear, may border on the ridiculous, too far removed from their daily reality.

Most of us have loved ones, family members and lifelong friends, who do not believe as we do. They do not know Jesus nor do they see the need for Him in their lives.

As believers, we know the eternal implications and the eternal importance of a life in Him. We have a responsibility to share the gospel, most especially with those we love.

For many of our loved ones we will be the greatest access to Jesus they have.

They may never open the Word of God or attend church. But they will see us and watch how we live out our lives - our real, ordinary, sometimes challenging daily lives.

In this, we have great opportunity and great responsibility. A responsibility that we cannot take lightly. Paul speaks of the unbeliever in 2 Corinthians 4:4 where he writes: *"In their case the god of this world has blinded the minds of the unbelievers, to keep them from seeing the light of the gospel of the glory of Christ, who is the image of God."* Many of us have loved ones whose minds are blinded; they are unable to see *"the light of the gospel of the glory of Christ."*

In fact, it was not that long ago that my own mind was blinded. I remember when I would read the Bible only to find fault and disagree with the words on the page. As Paul writes, my mind was dull and a veil covered my heart.

"But their minds were made dull, for to this day the same veil remains when the old covenant is read. It has not been removed, because only in Christ is it taken away. Even to this day when Moses is read, a veil covers their hearts. But whenever anyone turns to the Lord, the veil is taken away." 2 Corinthians 3:14-16 (NIV)

It was not until I turned to the Lord that the veil was taken away. I turned to the Lord in part because of a conversation initiated by my baby sister. I remember the day she asked "Who is Jesus to you?" From my answer, it was immediately apparent to her that I did not have a personal relationship with Jesus.

The question was not easy for her to ask; I am the oldest, a leader; she, the youngest, a follower. But I thank God, that on that day, she followed His leading and was brave enough to ask her big sister a difficult question. It would be many months and conversations later before I would finally come to know Christ for myself, but I can look back and see it all began with a question posed by my baby sister.

It is important that we share the gospel with those we love. But too often we think of sharing the gospel as witnessing, evangelizing, and preaching. While Jesus does say: *"Go and make disciples"* (Matthew 28:19), He also says to us: *"You are the light of the world."* (Matthew 5:14)

A light doesn't have to preach, a light simply shines.
- We are the light of the world. We are to shine.
- We are to shine so that others will see Jesus in us and through us.
- We shine by staying close to the light source. We stay plugged in to Him.
- We live in the Word and we live out the Word.
- We pray. Even when it's hard, especially when it's hard, we pray.
- We stand on the promises of Scripture:
    "The light shines in the darkness and the darkness has not overcome it." John 1:5 (ESV)

So, with Jesus in our hearts, we shine.

Diving Deeper

Read:

1. Read Philippians 2:14-16. Underline the things we are being instructed to do.

    "Do all things without grumbling or disputing, that you may be blameless and innocent, children of God without blemish in the midst of a crooked and twisted generation, among whom you shine as lights in the world, holding fast to the word of life, so that in the day of Christ I may be proud that I did not run in vain or labor in vain." (NASB)

    When we grumble and dispute with one another (or even within our own spirit) we obscure the light of Christ. How can we choose to be joyfully content in all things?

2. Read 1 Corinthians 1:9. *"Be careful, however, that the exercise of your rights does not become a stumbling block to the weak."* (ESV)

    How may your words or actions be a stumbling block in the path of a loved one coming to Christ? Ask God to search your heart and to show you in what way your light may shine brighter to draw that person to Christ.

Reflect and Relate:

1. In what way do you carry bitterness and resentment? What do you need to lay down so that the light of Christ may shine more brightly in you and through you? Ask God to show you how to decrease so that He may increase.

2. Who are your loved ones, family members and friends, who do not have a personal relationship with Christ? Write their names below and ask the Holy Spirit to give you individual Scripture to pray over each person's heart.

Prayer:

Dear God, I want to be a light who shines for you. Even if others can't name it or aren't sure what is different about me, may Jesus be seen in me. Please help me to humble myself and to get out of your way so that Jesus may shine through me. Please help me to decrease, so that He may increase in me. Please help me to love well. Please help me to live a life in which my actions speak louder than my words. Please help me to love well not only in word or talk but to love well in deed and in truth. Please help me to be a woman who not only loves your Word but a woman who lives out your Word so that others may see the Word through me. God, may I never forget - it is You who saves, I am simply meant to shine so that through me others may see you. In Jesus' holy and precious name I pray, Amen.

Prompt: For courage and an opportunity to share God's message with my family.

Praise:

For Others:

For Me:

Thanksgiving:

Let Your Soul be *Inspired*

DAY 22

Chosen to Proclaim His Excellence

By Michelle Nietert

> "But you are a chosen race, a royal priesthood, a holy nation, a people for his own possession, that you may proclaim the excellencies of him who called you out of darkness into his marvelous light."
>
> First Peter two : nine

Have you ever wanted something really really badly and not been chosen?

Maybe in school you wanted a certain class or teacher? Maybe you tried out for cheerleader or ran in an election and someone else was called "the fortunate one."

Maybe it's not you who experienced the disappointment or rejection but even worse you've suffered with one of your children who didn't make the team or get the part. Or sometimes even more devastating, you've experienced the recent heartbreak of loving someone and learned that they don't or no longer love you back.

Rejection can leave us aching and asking God, "Why not me?"

I recently sat in my counseling office with a young woman struggling with her appearance, intelligence and talent. She had high standards she felt she would never meet her own.

She had decided what she thought a beautiful woman looked like and it didn't include freckles which she had. She had decided that she wasn't smart enough to ever make a lot of money and she liked shopping – a lot.

She sat in my office tearful and lifeless as she felt she would never ever ever be good enough.

It's easy to write these feelings off to middle school angst. But if we're honest, in a culture that says how you look and what you do or have done is what makes you worthy of being chosen, we all struggle.

I think about the story of Jesus and the Samaritan woman at the well as told in John chapter four.

This woman was considered an outcast by His culture. She had made so many mistakes. I believe she must have felt that God would never interact with her or use her for His glory. Yet Jesus spoke to her, revealed Himself to her and then allowed her to be a witness to others.

In John 4:39, the scripture testifies to her work and its impact: "*Many of the Samaritans from that town believed in him because of the woman's testimony, 'He told me everything I ever did.'* (NIV).

In 1 Peter 2:9 it states that every single one of us who believes are a part of a chosen people, separate from the world.

> "But you are a chosen race, a royal priesthood, a holy nation,
> a people for his own possession, that you may proclaim the excellencies
> of him who called you out of darkness into his marvelous light." (ESV)

This scripture goes on to describe us as a people for his possession. It's amazing to think no matter how we feel we don't measure up in this world, we are God's.

Zephaniah 3:17 lets us know that God even delights in us and rejoices over us with singing.

> "The Lord your God is with you, the Mighty Warrior who saves.
> He will take great delight in you; in his love he will no longer rebuke you,
> but will rejoice over you with singing." (NIV)

I remember holding my babies in my arms so happy that they were mine and delighting in their tiny little faces. I would sometimes sing to them as they slept my heart full of joy. They didn't have to do one thing to be loved. I loved them because they were mine.

On tough days, when I feel like maybe I won't be chosen or life will never turn my way. I remind myself that God if He could would take me in His eternal arms, hold me and delight over me as I am just as I did with those sweet little babies of mine.

As we return to the verse in 1 Peter 2:9, we see the purpose or reason we are chosen and His. We are called to "*proclaim the excellencies of him who called you out of darkness into his marvelous light.*" (ESV)

When we realize His delight in us, just like that woman in Samaria, His love and the change it makes in us, we want others to know.

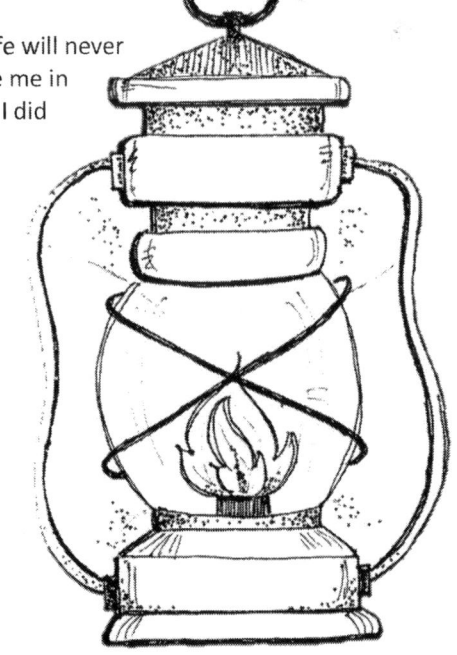

Let's proclaim to those around us, the greatness of the God who loves us.

Diving Deeper

Read:

1. Read again John 4:39. *"Many Samaritans from that town believed in him because of the woman's testimony, "He told me all that I ever did." (ESV)*

   What is the one thing the woman did?

   Why do you think she went back into the city to tell them about Jesus?

2. Read Ephesians 2:10. Circle or highlight the word used to describe you in the verse below.

   "For we are God's masterpiece. He has created us anew in Christ Jesus, so we can do the good things he planned for us long ago." (NLT)

   How would you describe a masterpiece?

   You were created on purpose and God has a plan for you. How can this truth help you when you are experiencing feelings of being less than or rejection?

Reflect and Relate:

1. Where are you today as you read these words? Have you ever felt less than or rejected? Maybe you do right now?

    How can knowing that God delights in you simply because you are His, help you deal with feelings of rejection?

2. Do you know someone else that needs to hear this message of acceptance? How would you tell them about the God who loves you and loves them?

Prayer:

Father in a world of high standards, sometimes it's so easy to feel less than and overlooked. I pray today that we would walk in the truth of who we are because we are Yours. We pray for those of us struggling with darkness that we would walk in marvelous of light of Your love. Show us today whom we could share it with in a world of darkness. In the name of Jesus, Amen.

Prompt: to recognize my true value in God's eyes

Praise:

For Others:

For Me:

Thanksgiving:

Let Your Soul Be Inspired

DAY 23

Actively Trusting
By Lauren Clark

> "And I will lead the blind in a way that they do not know, in paths that they have not known I will guide them. I will turn the darkness before them into light, the rough places into level ground. These are the things I do, and I do not forsake them."
>
> Isaiah forty-two : sixteen

On the weekends, I hit the Trinity trails in Lucas, Texas with my nine year-old, American Quarter horse, Bert. We have been going on the same trails for over 3 years now. The same dirt path lined by trees. The same two creeks with streaming water flowing through. The same hollowed tree log across the path. The same twists and turns, along the worn trail for the last 3 years. At first, Bert was constantly studying the trails for each new twist, turn, tree, creek, rock but after a while he became accustomed to these things and stopped expecting them – he stopped observing – he stopped studying. When he started to do this, I noticed that every little sound or noise would spook him more and it was because he was no longer paying attention.

Bert thought he knew the path and didn't need to be as aware and alert to what's ahead.

There were times that we would come to a fork in the road and instead of pushing forward he would try to turn around and head home. He knew that the path onward led further away and with that knowledge, he would fight my urging him to proceed. Bert became more accustomed to the trail and less willing to trust me to lead.

Do we do the same things with God?

Do we stop letting God lead us because we think we know what already lies ahead?

Do we become accustomed to our routines and less willing to trust Him to lead?

When we think we already know the way, it is harder to trust someone to lead. It is more difficult to let Him lead when we are in front. We get in the way of God when He is gently leading us. We let our ideas and perceptions of what it should look like keep us from following His promptings to move forward. We no longer become flexible and pliable to His promptings.

It says that He will turn "the rough places into level ground" but what if *we* are the rough places? We become the very thing that gets in the way of our future – *we become the rough spot in the road.*

Maybe it would be to our benefit not to trust our own sight but to act as if we were blind in order to be led! Yes, that might sound crazy but hear me out.

> If we are blind, we are truly dependent on Him to lead us. "***And I will lead the blind in a way that they do not know***" is the promise from our Savior in Isaiah. If we anticipate each next turn, we are not allowing Christ to lead us. In John 14:6 (ESV) it reads "***I am the way, and the truth, and the life. No one comes to the Father except through me***." He is the WAY! If He is the "Way" then I want Him to lead me in "the way". The path onward is through Him – the Way.

The path, the way, may be unfamiliar to us but it isn't to Him. He is leading us and our role is to trust Him. This is not a do-nothing role. Trust is an active role. It takes action on our part to trust. We can't be led if we are sitting and resistant. We must get up, trust and take His hand!

In Exodus 13:21-22 (ESV), it shows us that a promise was made to the people, God would lead them out of the wilderness and into the promise land. The people knew this promise but I am sure they were not anticipating to be led by a pillar of cloud by day and pillar of fire by night:

> "***The Lord went before them by day in a pillar of cloud to lead them along the way***
> ***and by night in a pillar of fire to give them light, that they might travel by day and by night.***
> ***The pillar of cloud by day and the pillar of fire by night did not depart from before the people.***"

God's people had never been led this way before – it was "a way they had not known" yet they followed His promptings and it brought them to the promise land.

Just like He led the Israelites and just like I lead Bert, God is leading each of us. It may not seem familiar but I would rather be on an unfamiliar path with God than a familiar path alone. We know that His ways are great than our ways and we reach out to take His hand today as He leads.

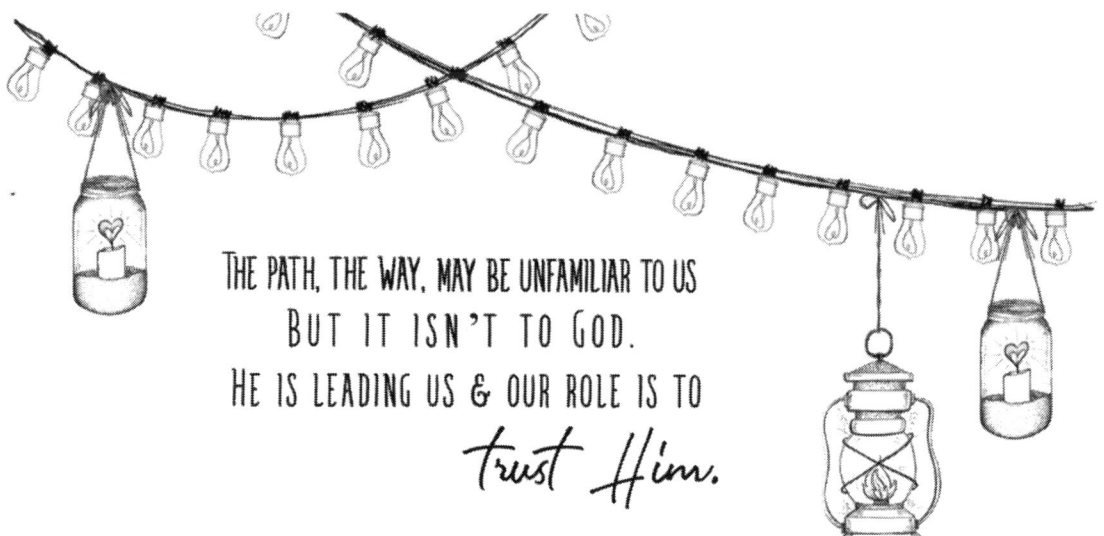

THE PATH, THE WAY, MAY BE UNFAMILIAR TO US
BUT IT ISN'T TO GOD.
HE IS LEADING US & OUR ROLE IS TO
trust Him.

Diving Deeper

Read:

1. Read Isaiah 55:8-9. *"For my thoughts are not your thoughts, neither are your ways my ways, declares the Lord. For as the heavens are higher than the earth, so are my ways higher than your ways and my thoughts than your thoughts."* (ESV)

   It can sometimes be difficult to discern God's path. Has there been a time in your life when you wanted to go one direction, but felt God leading you another? What did you do?

2. In 2 Corinthians 5:7, Paul states that *"for we walk by faith, not by sight."* (ESV), is there someone in your life you have witnessed walking by faith instead of sight? What did that look like?

Reflect and Relate:

1. Is there an area in your life, a current situation or struggle, where you may need to step out of the way and let God lead?

2. Which of the follow activities can you do to help you pro-actively trust God to lead you?

    - Seek Godly counsel confirming His leading.
    - Take time to pray.
    - Be still - open your ears to hear His promptings and direction for your life.
    - Write down scriptures that line up with where you are being led.
    - List areas and/or situations that you know you need to trust God.
    - List areas and/or situations you have trusted Him and how He has brought you through them.

3. Walking in faith is day by day and step by step, ask God for the courage to follow where He leads, step by step.

Prayer:
Lord, today we reach out our hand to grab yours. Lead us Lord! May we no longer trust in our own sight but actively trust in Yours, as you lovingly guide us. In Jesus' Name, Amen.

Prompt: Courage to follow where God leads

Praise:

For Others:

For Me:

Thanksgiving:

Let Your Soul be Inspired

DAY 24

When You Need a Light in the Darkness
By Betsy deCruz

> "SEND OUT YOUR LIGHT AND YOUR TRUTH; LET THEM LEAD ME; LET THEM BRING ME TO YOUR HOLY HILL AND TO YOUR DWELLING!"
>
> PSALM FORTY-THREE : THREE

When was the last time you experienced a power outage?

In the overseas country where I live, electricity cuts happen often. Everyday activities like cooking or taking a shower can be downright difficult in the dark. Most people in my city live in high rise buildings, and let me tell you, the worst part of a power outage is going down stairs.

Just the other evening, I had to go down six flights of stairs in the dark!

Scary when you're a clumsy woman like me who manages to fall down and hurt herself even by daylight. As I stood on the stairs looking into the blackness, fear almost paralyzed me. My husband and daughter were a few steps below me, but I couldn't see them.

The stairs had no handrail, but I was able to inch my way down by sliding my hand against the wall beside me and creeping my foot forward to feel the drop of each step.

Finally my husband got out his cell phone to shine light on the stairs.

A little light made all the difference. Fear left when I could see my way.

Sometimes life circumstances leave us feeling like we're groping in the dark, unsure of our way. You may be grieving the loss of a loved one, struggling to care for your children, or caught in an abusive relationship. Depression can set in when you can't see the way forward.

When life feels like a staircase in the dark, Psalm 43 offers a beautiful prayer:

"Send out your light and your truth;
let them lead me;
let them bring me to your holy hill
and to your dwelling!" Psalm 43:3 (ESV)

The Psalms are a book of prayers to read and make our own. When I feel downhearted, it helps to remember that the men and women of the Bible faced tough times too. We don't know what the writer of Psalm 43 was going through, but in verse 11 he wrote, *"Why, my soul, are you downcast? Why so disturbed within me?"* (NIV) It sounds to me like he was depressed.

How wonderful that today we can read his words and pray along with Him. This verse shows me three ways to pray through discouraging times.

Lord, send your light.
God's light dispels depression, renews hope and gives guidance. When life's challenges leave us unsure of our way, we can pray for God to shine His light on our path. He knows the way forward, and He'll show us each step we need to take.

Let your truth guide me.
When we're discouraged, we're susceptible to Satan's lies. Satan whispers to us: "Your situation is hopeless," "No one loves you," or "You're worthless." In God's Word, we find the truth: *"Nothing is impossible with God,"* *"Jesus gave his life for you,"* and *"You're fearfully and wonderfully made."*

The truth we find in the Bible gives us the encouragement and wisdom we need. I'm learning that when I take even ten minutes to read the Word each day, I find hope, comfort, and guidance for everything life throws my way.

Lead me to Yourself.
When the Psalmist prayed that God would lead him to His Holy dwelling, he was thinking of the temple in Jerusalem, where people went to meet with God. Because of the Holy Spirit's presence with believers, today we can meet God in our living rooms or on the walking trail.
A few minutes with Him can lift our spirits.

When I take time to listen to a worship song, pray, or read a portion of scripture, I remember how much God loves me, and I gain a new perspective on life. I see again how God is great enough to handle my problems.

When you feel down or unsure of your way, remember God has the light and truth you need. He wants nothing more than to lead you to Himself. We might not always know where we're going, but we can find comfort in remembering Who we're with.

A LITTLE *light* MADE ALL OF THE DIFFERENCE. FEAR LEFT WHEN I COULD SEE MY WAY.

Diving Deeper

Read:

1. In many ancient Hebrew manuscripts, Psalm 42 and 43 are one Psalm. One verse repeats itself three times in these Psalms. Let's listen to the Psalmist's self-talk:

   "Why, my soul, are you downcast?
   Why so disturbed within me?
   Put your hope in God,
   for I will yet praise him,
   my Savior and my God." Psalm 43:5 (NIV)

   What do these verses tell you about the writer's frame of mind?

   What can we learn from his words about how to react to hard times?

2. Read Psalm 42 and write down the verse you like best in the space provided below:

Reflect and Relate:

1. Take a few moments to consider what situations might be adding heaviness to your heart. List a few of these, and ask God to shine His light and give you His perspective on each one.

2. Do you have concerns or problems you don't know how to solve? Make a list of them and ask God to give you wisdom and guidance.

Prayer:

Lord, I praise you because you are the source of light and truth. Help me to look to you for hope and guidance today. In Jesus' name. Amen.

Prompt: A deeper desire to spend time with God

Praise:

For Others:

For Me:

Thanksgiving:

Let Your Soul be Inspired

John 12:36

DAY 25

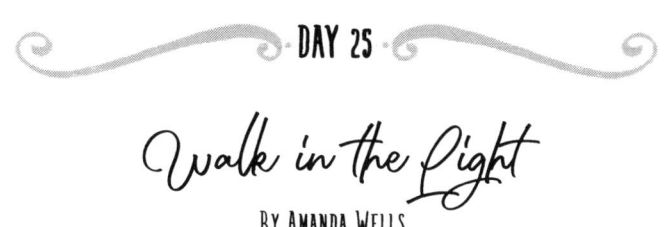

Walk in the Light
By Amanda Wells

> "So Jesus said to them, 'The light is among you for a little while longer. Walk while you have the light, lest darkness overtake you. The one who walks in the darkness does not know where he is going.'"
>
> John twelve : thirty-five

The leaves crunched beneath my feet as my flashlight's beam scanned the surrounding woods.

"Anyone there?" I asked, knowing there would be no answer in this competitive game of flashlight tag.

The light dimmed and I banged it against my leg, hoping to reignite the light but it faded until it disappeared completely. A nearby owl hooted. The leaves rustled as something darted through the trees, probably a squirrel. The moon hid behind the clouds and the darkness settled on my shoulders like a heavy weight. I couldn't see my hand in front of my face or the outline of trees that I knew were there. Goosebumps covered my arms but I refused to be scared.

I wouldn't let my fear of the dark overwhelm me tonight.

Have you ever been overwhelmed? Weighed down by past choices? Fearful because you couldn't see the path ahead of you or maybe fearful because its not the path you would have chosen?

When you're in this overwhelming place, it feels like the darkness is closing in on you? Maybe scared of the darkness itself like I was?

It's scary not seeing in front of you, the blindness causing uncertainty and unsure steps. The darkness engulfs us, seeking to oppress us.

You may not physically be in the dark but we can all experience dark places in our lives. Uncertainty of the future. Unsettled from changes. Uneasy with our choices.

With a dead flashlight battery and no backup, I was scared despite all outward shows of bravery.

I didn't like not knowing where to put my next step. I couldn't see where to go next and for all I knew, a hunting trap lay just ahead of me, ready to snap me up in captivity.

The light from a simple flashlight brought comfort because we see our surroundings and those things that felt so uncertain in the dark. In the glorious light illuminating those next few steps, lay the path we should take.

Jesus tells his disciples in John 12:35 to walk in the light before the darkness overtakes them because the one who walks in the darkness cannot see where he is going. He isn't referring to a flashlight or other source of light to brighten the darkness, but rather Himself.

These are some of the last words Jesus says, letting them know there is still time to turn to the light. The crowd could physically spend time with Jesus in person but He wanted them to know and trust Him even after He was gone.

John 8:12 says, *'Once again, Jesus spoke to the people and said, "I am the light of the world. Whoever follows me will never walk in darkness, but will have the light of life."* (xxx)

Do you have the light of life?

Are you spending your life in uncertainty and fear because you've been living in darkness?

Jesus says it doesn't have to be that way.

We might not be able to see Jesus face to face like his followers back then could, but we can still walk in His light. We can spend time reading the Bible and know Him better. And when we walk in His light, we become children of light, revealing the truth and pointing people to God.

Will you walk in the light today?

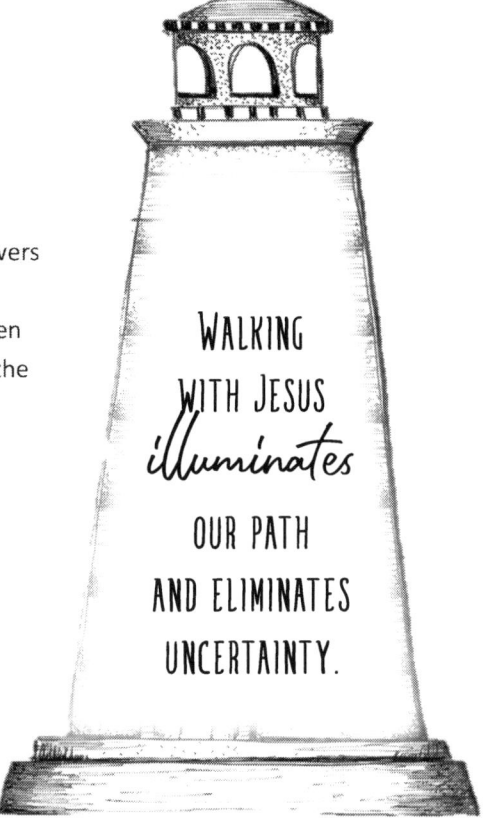

WALKING WITH JESUS illuminates OUR PATH AND ELIMINATES UNCERTAINTY.

Diving Deeper

Read:

1. Read Proverbs 4:19. *"The way of the wicked is like darkness; they do not know over what they stumble."* (ESV)

   Have you had a potential stumbling block in your path illuminated by God? What did His light reveal?

2. Read John 8:12 : "Again Jesus spoke to them, saying, "I am the light of the world. Whoever follows me will not walk in darkness, but will have the light of life.""" (ESV)

   How does God use each of these methods to shine His light into your life?

   The Scriptures:

   Prayer:

   Bible Teaching:

   What other methods does God use to shine His light?

Reflect and Relate:

1. If we walk in this light, we become children of light, revealing the truth and pointing people to God. How bright is your light? Can others see Jesus in you?

2. Are you walking on a path right now that needs some light for you to see you next step? Use the Scriptures to activate God's light. Look up some verses which relate to your situation. Write them out below.

Prayer:

Dear Lord, I've made some bad choices and I feel all alone, like I'm stranded in the dark and I don't know where to go from here. Forgive me for falling away from you and into the dark, shine you light on my life. Show me where to go from here and place people in my life to encourage me. Draw me nearer to you and illuminate your words as I read them in scripture. Be my light and help me point others to your. In Jesus' name, Amen.

Prayer Journal

Prompt: To not put off what needs to be done

Praise:

For Others:

For Me:

Thanksgiving:

Let Your Soul Be Inspired

DAY 26

Be the Light
By Jana Kennedy-Spicer

> "No one lights a lamp and puts it in a place where it will be hidden, or under a bowl. Instead they put it on its stand, so that those who come in may see the light."
>
> Luke eleven : thirty-three

I love burning candles in the house. Especially in the fall when I can fill the rooms with the sweet aroma of cinnamon and pumpkin spice. I typically keep candles if every room in the house just for decoration and enjoyment. I even have a couple of the old oil lamps used by my grandparents, they lived on farms with a lack of modern conveniences. But today, we are blessed with electricity so the candles and oil lamps no longer hold the utilitarian purpose for us that they once did.

But, that's in the fall; in the spring and summer, candles become more important. You see, we live in the country and when storms roll in, we often loose power. And why does this seem to happen most often in the evening?

So when the power goes out, the candles get lit for a more practical purpose. In the dark rooms, the candles are located where they will offer maximum illumination, especially in front of mirrors so the little candle light gets reflected across the room. Makes sense, right? I mean, why would I light a candle and put it in the closet or in a drawer?

Well, in verse 33 of the 11th chapter of Luke, Jesus is asking the same thing when He says, *"No one after lighting a lamp puts it in a cellar or under a basket, but on a stand; so those that enter may see the light."* (ESV)

As I studied today's scripture, I asked "who" is the light Jesus is speaking of? He is using a very practical example, but His teaching here has a much deeper meaning.

In John 8:12, Jesus says, *"I am the light of the world..."* but in the verses directly following Luke 11:33 (vs 35 & 36), Jesus talks about *"the light in you"* and *"your whole body is full of light"*.

So in verse 33 who is the light? I believe He is talking about the light within you and within me.

If we are the light, or lamp, what does this scripture tell us not to do? Don't hide the lamp away, don't put it in a place where it will not be seen.

I learned a couple of interesting things about the candle or lamp flame and these can be applied to why we are not to hide away.

1. **A flame needs oxygen to burn.**
   Oxygen is the flame's life source. So if a flame is lit but then hidden away without access to its life source, the flame will eventually extinguish itself, or go out. The candle or lamp will stop burning. Likewise, because the Holy Spirit is our internal flame, if we hide ourselves away and purposefully separate ourselves from our life source – God – then our internal flame can dim.

2. **A candle and lamp have a specific purpose.**
   They are lit to provide illumination; that's their job. A lamp that is lit then hidden away from sight, never fulfills its true purpose. It may still burn, but hidden away and alone, it provides no use to anyone.
   Likewise, we can also fail to fulfill our true purpose if after we have accepted Christ as our Lord and Savior we hide our faith away and never share it with others. (Acts 1:8)

Thankfully Jesus does not leave us hanging with just what we are not to do, if we look at the last half of Luke 11:33, He also shares with us what we *should do*.

In contrast to hiding, we are told that we are to put the light on display, on a stand. This is done so that the light source can be placed high and it can shine out above and over everything else, stretching its reach and shining as far as possible.

But let's be cautious just who we are putting on display – *ourselves or our light source, God Himself*.

In today's world of ministry, we hear the word "platform" a lot. It relates to how many followers one might have on social media. It represents someone's potential reach, how far they may be able to spread their message. But in the world of "platform building" it is very easy to switch one's focus from God to self.

I love the way a very dear friend put it, she said, "I don't want to build a bigger platform so more people can see me, I want to build a bigger light stand so more people can see God."

Soul Friends, let's bring our light up out of the cellar, let's cast aside those baskets holding back our internal light and let's fulfill the purpose assigned to us by God Himself, let's share Him with the world, let's *be the light*.

Read:

1. Read 1 Corinthians 6:19. *"Or do you not know that your body is a temple of the Holy Spirit within you, whom you have from God. You are not your own..."* (ESV)

    The Spirit of the Lord lives within each Christian, thus our body becomes a temple. How does knowing this impact how you take care of your body?

2. Read Acts 1:8, Christ's assignment for each of us. *"But you will receive power when the Holy Spirit come upon you, and you will be my witnesses in Jerusalem, and in all of Judea and Samaria and to the end of the earth."* (ESV)

    The reference to Jerusalem when applied to our lives, refers to our home town, home place, friends, family, co-workers, our close-in people.

    Write out Acts 1:8, personalizing it with your name and identifying your Jerusalem.

    What challenges might you need to overcome to *"be the light"* in your Jerusalem?

Reflect and Relate

1. What changes might you need to make to treat your body like the holy temple that it is?

2. Which of these things can you do to keep the flame of the Holy Spirit burning bright within? Ask God to reveal the answer to this question and add His directions to this list.

- Read the Bible
- Memorize Scripture
- Meditate on Scripture
- Spend time in prayer
-

- Spend time with God
- Study the Bible
- Listen to Bible based teaching / preaching
-
-

Prayer:

Father God, thank you for the gift of the Holy Spirit to lead and illuminate our lives from the inside out. I pray that my life can be a reflection of this holy light. Open the eyes of my heart to be aware of the people in my Jerusalem which need to hear your message. Thank you for these opportunities to be the light. In Jesus' Name, Amen.

Prompt: To put God in a place of honor in my life so others see Him, not me

Praise:

For Others:

For Me:

Thanksgiving:

Let Your Soul be Inspired

DAY 27

Looking For The Light
By Becky McCoy

> "The light shines in the darkness, and the darkness has not overcome it."
>
> — John One : Five

Have you ever felt like life is total darkness? I've felt that way often. When life is dark, it feels like you're living (or surviving) at the bottom of a pit with no hope of escape. Everywhere you turn, there's a wall, something keeping you from moving forward, out of the darkness.

When I was eight months pregnant, my husband died. I was the pregnant widow with the two year old at home. If I hadn't lived it, I would insist it was the storyline of a made-for-tv movie and not real life.

The day I left the hospital without my husband, my heart broke.

It broke because I wasn't going to spend the rest of my life with the man I loved and who loved me. It broke because there was a little boy at home who needed his daddy.

It broke because there was a little girl who wasn't even born yet who would never meet him.

The month after my husband died and before my daughter was born were total darkness. I remember lying in bed, staring at the ceiling, telling God he was wrong.

He didn't design families to be broken, but he let mine shatter.

Have you ever told God he was wrong? Maybe you watched a dream die or said goodbye to someone you love. Maybe you didn't lose something tangible or maybe you did. Really, what drove you into the darkness doesn't matter as much as what you decide to do in the darkness.

In the pit, are you digging in deeper or are you looking for the light?

According to John 1:4-5, Jesus is light. The life that he gives is the light that breaks through the darkness.

The verse continues to say that the darkness cannot overcome the light. 'Overcome', in the original Greek, means to comprehend, understand, or detect. Do you realize that Jesus is so full of life that the darkness cannot comprehend, understand, or detect him?

Our darkest hours don't magically disappear. Struggle remains and life can be so incredibly difficult. But how does your attitude towards struggle change when you realize that your darkest pit is not deeper than God's love for you?

Darkness is complicated.

God's love rescues me from the pit, but he doesn't require us to forget or ignore our hurting. He is full of compassion and grace and is not offended by our honest emotions. I love Psalm 40:1-2 and how God not only hears our cries and rescues us from our pit, but he puts our feet on solid, sturdy ground.

There's no darkness that is too much for God's love.

And God's love makes us more than conquerors. At the bottom of your darkest pit, you can cry out to God, he will hear you, and he will set you on sturdy ground. His love rescues you and gives you strength and courage.

YOUR DARKEST PIT IS NOT DEEPER THAN GOD'S LOVE FOR YOU.

Diving Deeper

Read:

1. Read Romans 8:37. *"No, in all these things we are more than conquerors through him who loved us."* (ESV)

    When you find yourself in a difficult situation, do you rely on your own strength or Gods?

    Think of a current or recent personal difficulty. In this situation, what would being a "conqueror" look like to you?

    What do you think being a "conqueror" would look like to God?

2. Read Psalm 40:1-2. *"I waited patiently for the Lord; he inclined to me and heard my cry. He drew me up from the pit of destruction, out of the miry bog, and set my feet upon a rock, making my steps secure."* (ESV)

    Do you find it difficult to wait? Even on God? Why is waiting so difficult?

    According to Psalm 40:1-2, what do we receive when we wait on God?

Reflect and Relate:

1. How have you seen the light of God's love during dark seasons of life?

2. What keeps you from accepting the strength and courage God offers us during times of struggle?

Prayer:

Dear God, thank you for loving me when I am unsure of you. Thank you for choosing to rescue me from my deepest, darkest pits and setting my feet on sturdy ground. Your love gives me strength and courage – help me choose to accept and look towards the light that is your love. In Jesus' name, Amen.

Prompt: To stand strong against the enemy

Praise:

For Others:

For Me:

Thanksgiving:

Let Your Soul Be Inspired

DAY 28

Not Invited to the Party
By Kristin Funston

> "And no wonder, for even Satan disguises himself as an angel of light."
>
> Second Corinthians eleven : fourteen

"Mama! Look! I'm a princess!"

My daughter twirled around in her costume, pink sparkles billowing out around her. She pranced off and spent the rest of the day ordering pretend servants around, inviting royal "guests" (Barbie and Ken dolls) to tea and doing whatever else it is three year old princesses do at fake dinner parties. I smiled and played along with the "princess" for a while, but then eventually grew tired of the game.

The acting through the tea party made me think ... just like my daughter masqueraded around that day, disguising her normal self as royalty, our enemy often does the same.

And quite frankly, I'm tired of his games too. What about you?

The difference between kids and our enemy dressing up is - clearly - a big one. Kids can't fool us. We are mature and discerning enough to see the evidence. I know my daughter is not actually royalty. She doesn't live in a castle, nor does she have servants at her beck and call (unless you count me, of course). She is unable to convince me she is actually a real-life princess.

However, Satan is much more sly.

In the New International Version, 2 Corinthians 11:14 tells us Satan "masquerades" himself.

It's a masquerade ... *a party.*

Satan loves deceiving us, and he enjoys himself when we fall for the lies. Isn't it funny (and appropriate) how the modern-day movies with a masquerade scene, most of the time, something awful happens? Murder, theft, or some other shade of darkness is hidden behind the masks. The darker the mask or costume, the darker the character.

This idea is as old as time ... that "light" means all things good, righteous, excellent and holy, while "dark" refers to evil, wrong, doom and gloom. It's a powerful example we've used for centuries.

We are, by human nature, lovers of light. Most things "dark" and evil aren't very appealing. So what better way to draw us into his lies, than for Satan hide behind his "light" mask?

One example of how he does this? Satan persuades us to do things under the name of religion, in order to distance us from God. The problem is, it is so hard to even realize it when it is happening.

- That ex we call and text just to be nice since he is having a hard time (without our husband knowing) ... because it's the Christian thing to do.
- That judgement cast on our homosexual neighbor ... in the name of Jesus.
- That alcoholic we enable ... since the Good Samaritan helped, we should too. (Luke 10:25-37).

Being nice, helpful and sharing Truth are all good things, but Satan is smart enough to use and twist good things into evil opportunities. He presents sin to us as something we should desire or need. He will also show false teaching as profound. He will do anything he can to distance us a little more from God. And he is ruthless.

"... Satan has demanded permission to sift you like wheat." Luke 22:31b (NASB)

I don't know about you, but this is almost discouraging. Hidden behind a mask, how are we able to see? Do we just hope he doesn't mess with us?

Friend, I can guarantee he'll mess with you in this way. I'm willing to bet he already has.

So how do we know when Satan has his ugly hands twisting our situation? How are we able to tell? Two ways ... (don't worry, they are relatively simple) ...

First, we must ask God for help.

If we ask Him, God will give us eyes to see and wisdom to discern what is from Him and what is not. He desperately wants us to know, so nothing comes between us and Him. So we can be assured it is in His will that our questions will be answered.

Second, we must read His word.

The only way to understand what is of God is to get to know Him. We do this through prayer and reading the Bible. It's the only way we can battle the enemy and plan to come out on top.

Evil is scary. But there's Good News. Satan didn't, isn't and can't win. Jesus has already defeated him and we can celebrate with our Savior.

Even though there is evil masked as good, God is always good.

And that's a party I want to celebrate at ... but Satan's not invited this time.

Diving Deeper

Read:

1. Read John 14:13-14. *"Whatever you ask in My name, that will I do, so that the Father may be glorified in the Son. "If you ask Me anything in My name, I will do it."* (NASB)

    What do you need to ask God for to assist you in recognizing the devil's lies and schemes?

2. Read 2 Timothy 3:16. *"All Scripture is God-breathed and is useful for teaching, rebuking, correcting and training in righteousness…"* (NIV)

    Spending time in God's Word is our best defense against the devil's schemes. What keeps you from reading the Bible?

    What might you need to change so you can spend time on a regular basis reading God's Word?

Reflect and Relate:

1. Ephesians 6 lists out the armor God provides us. Circle the pieces of armor listed in scripture.

   "Therefore put on the full armor of God, so that when the day of evil comes, you may be able to stand your ground, and after you have done everything, to stand. Stand firm then, with the belt of truth buckled around your waist, with the breastplate of righteousness in place, and with your feet fitted with the readiness that comes from the gospel of peace. In addition to all this, take up the shield of faith, with which you can extinguish all the flaming arrows of the evil one. Take the helmet of salvation and the sword of the Spirit, which is the word of God." Ephesians 6:11-17 (NIV)

   List out below the pieces of armor you feel you have forgotten to strap on in previous battles. List ways to help you remember these pieces for your next battle with the enemy.

2. *"The thief comes only to steal and kill and destroy. I came that they may have life and have it abundantly."* John 10:10 (ESV)

   List 3 scenarios or situations you've seen Satan at work. Then list 3 scenarios or situations you have seen God offer abundant life.

   1.   1.

   2.   2.

   3.   3.

Prayer:

Lord, we humbly come to your throne of grace in our time of need. The enemy is sneaky and often hard to recognize. Give us eyes to recognize him and the wisdom to know how to handle the situation he is trying to manipulate. We know You have already won the battle, and we praise You. Thank you, God. In Jesus' Name, Amen.

Prompt: To recognize the true enemy

Praise:

For Others:

For Me:

Thanksgiving:

Let Your Soul be Inspired

DAY 29

Stuck on the Bathroom Floor

By Lindsey Alexander

> "For you have delivered my soul from death, yes, my feet from falling, that I may walk before God in the light of life."
>
> Psalm fifty-six : thirteen

I am not sure when this memory will fade. Right now, it is as vivid as it can be.

My family had a wonderful day that day. I had already changed into my pajamas and washed my face as I was preparing for bed. It was then that it hit me. This sharp and stabbing pain in my stomach. It wouldn't let go and I found myself becoming afraid as the pain became unrelenting. I was by myself in the bathroom and tried to take a few deep breaths to calm the fears that were now coming over me.

"Am I having a heart attack?"

I yelled for my husband as I fell to my knees on the bathroom floor. The pain in my stomach was now radiating down my right arm and within seconds I lost all function of my right side.

"Am I having a stroke?"

My husband walked into the bathroom and found me with tears streaming down my face in a twisted and contorted ball. I could not move. He attempted to lift me into the hallway and I screamed in pain. I had little control over my body and this foreign state I found myself in was creating a panic for us both.

"Call 911," I yelled. "What is happening to me?"

As my husband was on the phone with the EMS dispatch I began praying out loud to my Father.

"God, please help me! I don't know what's happening to me, but I know that you do. Lord, help me to trust you, even though I am afraid."

My body was shaking uncontrollably and it felt like an hour before the ambulance pulled into our driveway. I was loaded onto a gurney, given an IV and we began the trek to the hospital.

What followed was an entire night in the emergency room completing test after test in attempt to figure out what had happened to me. My pain subsided throughout the evening and I started to wonder if the whole night had just been a really bad dream. I was discharged in the morning and sent home with an "inconclusive" diagnosis.

In the weeks to follow, I had several more tests and meetings with doctors and it was in a meeting with my GI doctor that the reality of my painful evening was placed before me. My doctor looked me in the eyes and tenderly said, "Sometimes Lindsay, our bodies react externally to something happening internally. I truly believe that you had a massive panic attack that night."

I was in shock. A panic attack?

I really felt like I was navigating life okay and that my hands were wide open…but if I was being honest with myself, I was white knuckling life to death. My palms were not up in total surrender; they were facing the right direction but my fists were clinched shut.

My heart began to break in a really cool way. I continually felt God speaking over me.

> "*I have more for you Lindsay.* I have a life planned that will blow your mind
> if you open those hands wide. When you prayed to me on that bathroom floor,
> *I heard every single word.* I will help you to trust me, even though you are afraid.
> I will sustain you and carry you every single day."
> ~ God ~

I would love to tell you that my hands were spread wide open overnight but the truth is that God lovingly uncurled each finger as He covered me in grace and new mercies each day.

He showed me that the measure to which he can use me is directly proportional to how open my hands are.

He guided me to safe and prosperous ground.

He delivered me from that bathroom floor to a life of excited abandon as I reside and abide under His mighty and powerful wing minute by minute.

Have you been there too? Caught in the thick of it and stuck on the bathroom floor?

He hears you and he sees you. He is close to your hurt, your heartache, your struggle. He can be trusted with your fears and your clinched fists.

Let your Heavenly Father lovingly loosen your grip one finger at a time. It is then that you can boldly walk forward in gratitude, faith and hope.

Diving Deeper

Read:

1. Read 2 Corinthians 1:10. *"He delivered us from such a deadly peril, and he will deliver us. On him we have set our hope that he will deliver us again."* (ESV)

    Can you recall a time when God delivered you from a difficult situation or circumstance?

    How can recalling this moment of deliverance give you hope in the next trial?

3. Read Isaiah 46:4. List a few ways that God is sustaining you in this season of life.

    "Even to your old age I am he, and to gray hairs I will carry you. I have made, and I will bear; I will carry and will save." (ESV)

Reflect and Relate:

1. Would you say that you are living with your hands open or your hands in fists?

    - If you do feel like your life is open handed, what areas of your life do you find yourself tightening your grip again? Ask God to help you release that area to him.

    - If you feel your fists are clinched, write down the areas of your life where you need to relinquish control and allow God to work through you.

2. God is called the "Devine Deliverer." He is the only one who can truly free us from our spiritual decline and guide us towards a better way. What do you need delivering from today?

Prayer:
Heavenly Father, thank you that when we cry out you hear us. That we can rest in assurance that you will deliver us from our troubles. Show us when our fists are clinching yet again so that we can walk in the light and be used for your glory and our own good. In your Perfect Name we pray, Amen.

Prompt: To walk in a manner pleasing to God

Praise:

For Others:

For Me:

Thanksgiving:

Let Your Soul be Inspired

DAY 30

Practically Perfect in Every Way
By Tina Gibson

> "THE PEOPLE WHO WALKED IN DARKNESS HAVE SEEN A GREAT LIGHT. THOSE WHO DWELT IN A LAND OF DEEP DARKNESS ON THEM HAS LIGHT SHONE."
>
> ISAIAH NINE : TWO

As a little girl, my favorite movie was Mary Poppins. I loved every (perfect) thing about her. In fact, there's a scene in the movie where she pulls a tape measure out of her (perfect) bag to measure the height of the children she was caring for, Jane and Michael Banks. Instead of numbers, the readings were personality traits like stubborn or prone to giggle. But for her, it read: "Mary Poppins, practically perfect in every way."

Right on, Mary. Right on.

In my world, perfection was always the prize. Perfect daughter. Perfect friend. Perfect student. Perfect date. Perfect employee. Perfect-a-mundo.

Not.

When I was 23 years old, my perfect little world fell apart. My Dad was dying and quite frankly, so was I. Not physically, but emotionally. My family of Dad, Mom, and I were threatened by a cancer with an uncontrollable outcome. So, consciously or not, I chose to control the only thing that I could.

Me.

And that was reflected in my eating. I went from a lover of cheeseburgers and fries to a lover of salads. Sounds healthy, right? Well, that full salad went to a half salad that went to "I'll just have a bite or two, I'm full" salad.

As my body changed to reflect that, I translated the concerned comments of "You've lost a lot of weight…" to mean "Wow, keep up the good work!" You see, I controlled the way I heard their words and interpreted them into what I wanted to hear.

Perfection.

Looking back now, I realize that the bags of groceries my folks sent home with me reflected their desperate desire to help. My well-meaning friends would invite me for pizza parties or late night ice cream runs...but I never went.

I just didn't feel like it. I wasn't healthy and neither was my heart. It fluttered. It hurt. It felt weak, tired, less than perfect. *And so did I.*

During this time, I didn't talk to God much. Oh, I grew up in the church. I knew Jesus as my personal Savior. But, I had stepped into a period of darkness that I chose to control. Honestly, I'm not sure why. Was I was mad at God because my Dad was dying? Only He knows for sure.

Yet, although my prayers were few, the love of my Heavenly Father for me was fierce. He carried me when I didn't even know it. And He ultimately brought me to an unlikely place where my need to be perfect received a reality check.

Waldenbooks. I had always enjoyed a bookstore, so it's no surprise that I went inside. But, I wasn't prepared for the magazine cover that changed everything. The headline announcing the death of a famous singer read something like this: Dead at 33. Heart Failure caused by Anorexia Nervosa. I picked it up and started reading. Her story and her symptoms mirrored mine.

At that moment, I felt a wave of fear cover me. Not the fear of living, but the fear of dying. And I immediately let go of my control and all things perfection and cried out in my soul with desperation.

Dear God Help me please!

I wish I could tell you that I went back home that day and ate a three course meal with dessert. But I can't. It took time for my body and my spirit to heal. It took the intentional letting go of me to the only One who could set me free.

One day at a time.

What about you, friend? Do you wrestle with the need to be practically perfect in every way? Are you fearful about letting go of control and letting God direct your steps? I so understand.

Dear one, whatever you fear today, God is bigger. He made you one of a kind and loves you just the way you are. Let His Perfect Love pour over you and heal your broken heart, wipe away your insecurities, and free you from darkness.

I still have moments where I try to be "practically perfect in every way". But, I don't linger there. Instead, I choose the light instead of the darkness and remind myself that I am enough...that He is enough.

Diving Deeper

Read:

1. Read Colossians 1:13-14. Circle the words which indicate God's action toward us.

    "For he has rescued us from the dominion of darkness and brought us into the kingdom of the son he loves; in whom we have redemption, the forgiveness of sins." (NIV)

    How has God acted in these ways in your own life?

2. In Psalm 27:1, David is making a declaration that he will no longer be afraid because God is his stronghold. As you read the scripture, ask God to reveal to you areas in your life where fear has overtaken your faith in God. List one or two areas where you sense God leading you to face and lay down those fears.

    "The Lord is my light and my salvation—whom shall I fear? The Lord is the stronghold of my life—of whom shall I be afraid?" (NIV)

Reflect and Relate:

1. In what areas of your life do you struggle to be perfect or to be in control?

2. Ask God to shine His light into your heart and reveal the fear hiding below your need for perfection in the area(s) of your life you listed.

3. Give these fears to Jesus right now and ask Him to help you. He loves you so much!

Prayer:
Father God, Thanks for loving us, not because we are perfect, but because You are perfect. Hold us close and fill us your peace and hope today. In Jesus' Name, Amen.

Prompt: to shine God's light into someone's darkness

Praise:

For Others:

For Me:

Thanksgiving:

Let Your Soul Be *Inspired*

DAY 31

No More Darkness
By Jana Kennedy-Spicer

> "And night will be no more. They will need no light of lamp or sun, for the Lord God will be their light, and they will reign forever and ever."
>
> Revelation twenty-two : five

Revelation. Chapter 22. The last chapter of the last book in the Bible.

A lot of us tend to shy away from the book of Revelation. It is full of end-times actives, angels, heaven, books with seals, and rich in symbolism that even Biblical scholar's don't always agree on. It can be a tough study.

But for us, I think today's scripture is the perfect verse to wrap up our 31 days of learning how to let our light shine.

In Revelation 22:5, John is actually revealing to us three truths about what the angel of the Lord has shared with him about Heaven and the scene surrounding the crystal river of life flowing from the throne of God. So let's unpack our scripture and take a look at each truth separately.

"And the night will be no more"

We've learned through our study that when the Bible mentions darkness it can mean 1) a literal absence of light or 2) an absence of God, or 3) a presence of evil, something harmful or unholy,

In this verse, all three of these scenarios actually apply.

In Heaven, there will be
- A literal absence of darkness
    1. Revelation 21:25 – there will be no night
- A figurative absence of darkness
    1. Revelation 21:4 – no mourning, pain or death
    2. Revelation 21:7 – nothing evil, impure or unclean
    3. Revelation 22:3 – nothing accursed (doomed, condemned, unholy)

And why will there be no darkness in Heaven?

"they will need no light of lamp or sun for the Lord God will be their light"

During our study we've learned of many ways God is a figurative light in our lives right now as we live here on Earth.

But in Heaven, He will become a literal light, driving out all darkness.
- Revelation 21:23 – glory of God gives light
- Revelation 21:11 – God's radiance is like a jewel

Oh what a spectacular image that will be! To look into the holy face of our God.

As Moses stood in the very real presence of God, in conversation with Him, he was told, *"'but', he [God] said, 'you can not see my face, for man shall not see me and live.'"* Exodus 33:20 (ESV)

Being in God's presence and not looking at Him was just too much for Moses, so as God was leaving, God gave him a glance at His glory (Exodus 33:19-23) and Moses was so transformed by this momentary exposure to God that he had to wear a veil to cover his face when he went back among the people. (Exodus 34:29-33)

So you can just imagine God's radiant glory fully exposed to those in Heaven and in their transformation becoming literal lights reflecting the glory of God.

There is no wonder there will be no need for a sun or moon!

"And they will reign forever and ever"

Eternity in heaven with God is what we receive when we accept the gift of salvation through Jesus Christ. (Romans 5:17)

But we are also told that there will be ones who reign, or rule, side by side with God in Heaven.
- Revelation 20:24 – the martyrs of the tribulation will be seated in authority
- 2 Timothy 2:12 – those who endure persecution will reign with God
- Daniel 7:27 – the dominions (lands, territories) will serve the saints in heaven

An eternity in Heaven with God, in His service, no more darkness, pain, anguish, and the incomprehensible splendor of God's glory illuminating the heavens.

Oh my. Compared with our earthly woes, some days I just can't wait.

But there is one more thing we need to take notice of in today's scripture, one little word that makes all of the difference between witnessing this heavenly sight or not – *they*.

John specifically states *"they will"*. There is most definitely a specific people identified with and assigned to experiencing the truth of this verse.

Sometimes we make the mistake of reading a verse in the Bible and automatically applying it to ourselves. While there may be a lesson for us to learn, every scripture and promise does not necessarily apply to every person. So it is important for us to learn who is the "they" John is speaking of.

Does it include you and me?

You see, this spectacular heavenly sight is not for everyone. There are two groups of people, the "*they*" that will witness God's glory eternally and the "*they*" that will not.

Interestingly, when the angel of God was making the heavenly revelations to John, even he asked the angel, "*who are these?*" (Revelation 7:13).

In this scripture, "they" are the ones who are
- Revelation 22:3 – His [God's] servants
- Revelation 7:15 – bondservants to [God's] throne
- Revelation 7:13 – cleansed by the blood of Jesus

"*They*" are the saved by Christ. "*They*" are the ones who have accepted the free gift of God's grace which has been offered to us from Jesus Christ through the shedding of His blood to blot out our sins.

"*They" are not everyone.*

It is very important to note, no, *it is the most important thing to note*, that only those cleansed by Christ's blood will experience the truth John reveals to us in Revelation 22:5.

Will this be you? Can you reread today's scripture, substituting your name for "*they*" and it be true?

If so, hallelujah!

If not, or if you're not sure, I invite you to go back and reread day one of our devotional, and talk to God about accepting His free gift of salvation.

Diving Deeper

Read:

1. Read Revelation 22:3. *"No longer will there be anything accursed, but the throne of God and of the Lamb will be in it, and his servants will worship him." (ESV)*

    How does knowing that there will be no darkness (anything accursed, unholy) in Heaven, help you deal with those things here on Earth?

2. Read Revelation 22:14-15. *"Blessed are those who wash their robes, so that they may have the right to the tree of life and that they may enter the city by the gates. Outside are the dogs and sorcerers and the sexually immoral and murderers and idolaters, and everyone who loves and practices falsehood." (ESV)*

    Who will be able to enter into the city gates, into Heaven?

    Who will not?

Reflect and Relate:

1. If you could share with someone how God shines His light into your life, what would you tell them?

2. Is there anyone in your life you are unsure about being part of the "they" ?

    How could our open the door to share the message of God's grace and forgiveness with them?

Prayer:

Dear Lord, we thank you for the beautiful glimpse into heaven, that there will be a day when those redeemed by Christ's blood can live eternally in the light of your glory and grace. I pray for each woman reading this today Lord, that in their heart they have received your gift of forgiveness. I ask forgiveness for the all the times I have failed to be a reflector of your light, and I ask you to make me more aware of the opportunities to share the message of your love and grace with others. Until that day that I can spend eternity in your presence, I ask these things In Jesus' name, Amen.

Prompt: To maintain perspective of this temporary home

Praise:

For Others:

For Me:

Thanksgiving:

Let Your Soul Be Inspired

Praying Scripture

Using the Bible to Grow Your Prayer Life

Becoming A Prayer Warrior
By Jana Kennedy-Spicer

Prayer.

I have to admit that this word has always intimidated me. I spent many years feeling inadequate and unworthy to come before God with my petitions; fumbling through the right words, careful to try and say just the right thing; for some reason thinking I had to silently pray in the "King James Version". It was a struggle, so I would find myself there only as a last resort.

I spent so much time thinking that prayer was just a way to ask God for what I wanted, never understanding that prayer served a much greater purpose. Never really grasping that God loves me and wants to have a relationship with me! Of course, to build a relationship takes spending time with each other and takes communication. Prayer.

Prayer warrior or prayer wimp?

Hello, I'm Jana, and I'm a prayer wimp.

In Max Lucado's book "*Before Amen*"[1] he starts off with this,
"*Hello, my name is Max. I'm a recovering prayer wimp. I doze off when I pray. My thoughts zig, then zag, then zig again. Distractions swarm like gnats on a summer night. If attention deficit disorder applies to prayer, I am afflicted. When I pray, I think of a thousand things I need to do. I forget the one thing I set out to do. Pray.*"

That is SO me!

And I must admit that it is a bit comforting to know that a pastor and man of God such as Max struggles with prayer also.

There is hope for me! And friend if you're saying, "yea, that sounds like me too", then know that here is hope for you too!

A conversation.

He also goes on to tell us that, "prayer is simply a heartfelt conversation between God and His child." A conversation... personal, confidential, mutual. This helps me, just be me, just talk to God. And this has made a difference for me with my prayers.

Oh I still have struggles, I am not where I want to be and not where I need to be with my prayer life. But with the help of God, I am not where I used to be. Progress.

How about you, would you like to become a prayer warrior? I hope so. I've also invited my Soul Friend Betsy to join us on our journey and share about how she incorporates the Bible into her prayer life.

[1] *Before Amen: The Power of a Simple Prayer* by Max Lucado, © Thomas Nelson 2014

Praying God's Word
By Betsy DeCruz

Do you ever feel unsure of how to pray for someone you love? Have you ever gotten tired of praying the same things day in and day out? Does your mind wander while you're trying to talk to God?

Friend, you're not alone. I'm the queen of distraction, so I've experienced all of these. I want to grow closer to God and see lives changed through prayer, yet my mind can travel to the moon and back when I try to pray. That's why I want to learn more about using God's Word to fuel and focus my conversation with Him.

Scripture works like a springboard for prayer. As we read it, the Holy Spirit sparks our thoughts and leads us into closer communion with Him.

Praying God's Word has several benefits:

- **It gives direction to our prayer.** When we don't know how to pray for a person or situation, scripture shows us. We know we're praying in line with God's will when we pray His very words back to Him. And when we're left speechless at the end of our rope, it gives us the words we need.

- **God's Word has power.** Scripture has authority. It's alive and active. It's a mighty weapon of spiritual warfare that fuels our faith and breaks down strongholds. We find power when we pray God's inspired Word.

- **God's Word is an anchor.** When your mind wanders, you can always go back to the scripture that sparked your prayer. When your faith flounders, the Bible gives you words to declare and something to stand on.

Here are Three Ways Pray Using Scripture:

1. **Pray God's Word in Your Quiet Time**
   In your devotional reading, respond to God's words by praying them back to Him. After you read a passage, go back and read it again, pausing to respond to God when you see a verse that sparks prayer.
   Look for the following
   ⇒ A quality or action you can praise God for.
   ⇒ A blessing to thank Him for.
   ⇒ Something you want to ask God for.

2. **Use memory verses as prayer prompts.**
   If you're using a scripture memory program, spend a few minutes praying through a verse after you review it. Lift up to God whatever thoughts come to mind. Perhaps you'll want to pray for yourself or for a loved one, asking for grace to obey a command, or faith to believe a promise.

3. Pray Along with the prayers of the Bible
   God's Word contains the most beautiful and powerful prayers ever written. Pray along with the people of the Bible as they wrestle with God, praise Him, and bring their petitions before Him.

   Here are several prayers from scripture you can make your own:
   ⇒ 1 Chronicles 29:10-13
   ⇒ Psalm 51
   ⇒ Luke 1:46-55
   ⇒ Ephesians 1:15-23
   ⇒ Ephesians 3: 14-21
   ⇒ Colossians 1: 9-12

As you pray more of God's Word, your faith will grow. When your words echo His, you grow closer to Him. Soul friends, here's something you can try right now before you go:

Read the *Let Your Light Shine* verse below:

"This is the message we have heard from him and proclaim to you, that God is light, and in him is no darkness." 1 John 1:5

Do you know someone who needs to know this right now? Stop a moment to pray for that person and praise God for His guiding light.

Praying Scripture

I loved this idea of praying scripture so much that I did the same for my family and below are some of the scriptures I try to pray regularly over each one of them.

For children, Colossians 1:9-14, (ESV)
"And so, from the day we heard, we have not ceased to pray for you, asking that you may be filled with the knowledge of his will in all spiritual wisdom and understanding, so as to walk in a manner worthy of the Lord, fully pleasing to him, bearing fruit in every good work and increasing in the knowledge of God. May you be strengthened with all power, according to his glorious might, for all endurance and patience with joy, giving thanks to the Father, who has qualified you to share in the inheritance of the saints in light. He has delivered us from the domain of darkness and transferred us to the kingdom of his beloved Son, in whom we have redemption, the forgiveness of sins."

For married couples, Romans 15:5-6, (ESV)
"May the God of endurance and encouragement grant you to live in such harmony with one another, in accord with Christ Jesus, that together you may with one voice glorify the God and Father of our Lord Jesus Christ."

For men, Ephesians 6:11-18, (ESV)
"Put on the full armor of God so that you can take your stand against the devil's schemes. For our struggle is not against flesh and blood, but against the rulers, against the authorities, against the powers of this dark world and against the spiritual forces of evil in the heavenly realms. Therefore put on the full armor of God, so that when the day of evil comes, you may be able to stand your ground, and after you have done everything, to stand. Stand firm then, with the belt of truth buckled around your waist, with the breastplate of righteousness in place, and with your feet fitted with the readiness that comes from the gospel of peace. In addition to all this, take up the shield of faith, with which you can extinguish all the flaming arrows of the evil one. Take the helmet of salvation and the sword of the Spirit, which is the word of God. And pray in the Spirit on all occasions with all kinds of prayers and requests. With this in mind, be alert and always keep on praying for all the saints."

For women, Proverbs 31:25-31, (ESV)
"Strength and dignity are her clothing, and she laughs at the time to come. She opens her mouth with wisdom, and the teaching of kindness is on her tongue. She looks well to the ways of her household and does not eat the bread of idleness. Her children rise up and call her blessed; her husband also, and he praises her: "Many women have done excellently, but you surpass them all." Charm is deceitful, and beauty is vain, but a woman who fears the Lord is to be praised. Give her of the fruit of her hands, and let her works praise her in the gates."

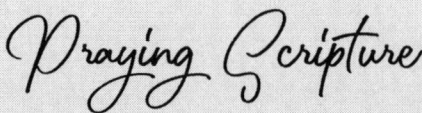

Praying Scripture

For parents, Ephesians 1:1-20, (ESV)
"because I have heard of your faith in the Lord Jesus and your love toward all the saints, I do not cease to give thanks for you, remembering you in my prayers, that the God of our Lord Jesus Christ, the Father of glory, may give you the Spirit of wisdom and of revelation in the knowledge of him, having the eyes of your hearts enlightened, that you may know what is the hope to which he has called you, what are the riches of his glorious inheritance in the saints, and what is the immeasurable greatness of his power toward us who believe, according to the working of his great might that he worked in Christ when he raised him from the dead and seated him at his right hand in the heavenly places"

For spouses, I Corinthians 13:4-13, (ESV)
"Love is patient and kind; love does not envy or boast; it is not arrogant or rude. It does not insist on its own way; it is not irritable or resentful; it does not rejoice at wrongdoing, but rejoices with the truth. Love bears all things, believes all things, hopes all things, endures all things. Love never ends. As for prophecies, they will pass away; as for tongues, they will cease; as for knowledge, it will pass away. For we know in part and we prophesy in part, but when the perfect comes, the partial will pass away. When I was a child, I spoke like a child, I thought like a child, I reasoned like a child. When I became a man, I gave up childish ways. For now we see in a mirror dimly, but then face to face. Now I know in part; then I shall know fully, even as I have been fully known. So now faith, hope, and love abide, these three; but the greatest of these is love."

For friends, Ephesians 3:14-19 (ESV)
"For this reason I bow my knees before the Father, from whom every family in heaven and on earth is named, that according to the riches of his glory he may grant you to be strengthened with power through his Spirit I your inner being, so that Christ may dwell in your hearts through faith—that you, being rooted and grounded in love, may have strength to comprehend will all the saints what is the breadth and length and height and depth, and to know the love of Christ that surpasses knowledge, that you may be filled with all the fullness of God."

For me, Luke 1:46-55 (ESV)
"And Mary said, my soul glorifies the Lord and my spirit rejoices in God my Savior, for he has been mindful of the humble state of his servant. From now on all generations will call me blessed, for the Mighty One has done great things for me—holy is his name. His mercy extends to those who fear him, from generation to generation. He has performed mighty deeds with his arm; he has scattered those who are proud in their inmost thoughts. He has brought down rulers from their thrones but has lifted up the humble. He has filled the hungry with good things but has sent the rich away empty. He has helped his servant Israel, remembering to be merciful to Abraham and his descendants forever, just as he promised our ancestors."

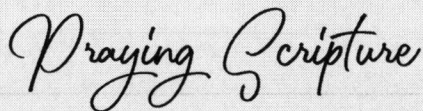

Praying Scripture

What things do you pray for in your own life? Knowledge, understanding, peace? Here are some scriptures by topic you could include in your prayer time.

Confidence: 2 Corinthians 3:4-6 (ESV)
"Such is the confidence that we have through Christ toward God. Not that we are sufficient in ourselves to claim anything as coming from us, but our sufficiency is from God, who has made us sufficient to be ministers of a new covenant, not of the letter but of the Spirit. For the letter kills, but the Spirit gives life."

Forgiveness (giving): Matthew 6:14-15 (ESV)
"For if you forgive others their trespasses, your heavenly Father will also forgive you, but if you do not forgive others their trespasses, neither will your Father forgive your trespasses."

Repentance: Psalm 51 (whole chapter) (ESV)
"Have mercy on me, O God, according to your steadfast love; according to your abundant mercy blot out my transgressions. Wash me thoroughly from my iniquity, and cleanse me from my sin!"

Attitude: Colossians 2:12-13 (ESV)
"Put on then, as God's chosen ones, holy and beloved, compassion, kindness, humility, meekness and patience, bearing with one another and , if one has a complaint against another, forgiving each other, as the Lord has forgiven you, so you also must forgive."

Thanksgiving: 1 Chronicles 16:34 (ESV)
"Oh give thanks to the LORD, for he is good; for his steadfast love endures forever!"

Endurance: Hebrews 12:1-2 (ESV)
"Therefore, since we are surrounded by so great a cloud of witnesses, let us also lay aside every weight, and sin which clings so closely, and let us run with endurance the race that is set before us, looking to Jesus, the founder and perfecter of our faith, who for the joy that was set before him endured the cross, despising the shame, and is seated at the right hand of the throne of God."

Peace Keeping: Titus 3:1-2 (ESV)
"Remind them to be submissive to rulers and authorities, to be obedient, to be ready for every good work, to speak evil of no one, to avoid quarreling, to be gentle, and to shop perfect courtesy toward all people."

Worry: Philippians 3:6-7 (ESV)
"Do not be anxious about anything, but in everything by prayer and supplication with thanksgiving let your requests be made known to God. And the peace of God, which surpasses all understanding, will guard your hearts and your minds in Christ Jesus"

Daily Prayer Prompts

Sometimes the hardest part of praying is knowing where to begin. So to assist you, as you are working through your daily Let Your Light Shine Devotional, you will find a section to incorporate prayer into your study time. It includes a prayer from each author as well as space to write out your own prayer.

I encourage you to include the day's scripture into your prayer, seeking God's guidance about 1) what God is wanting to teach you from the scripture and 2) how you can incorporate the learning into your life. Secondly, use the daily prayer prompts provided below to pray over others in your life.

Also included on the following pages are blank prayer journaling pages. Use these for additional space to write our your prayers. Feel free to make additional copies of those blank pages for your prayer time. Tuck them into your devotional, Bible, journal or notebook.

Day 1	boldness to be a witness for Christ
Day 2	for those suffering through hardships
Day 3	for God to open the door to be an encouragement to someone
Day 4	strength to break bad habits
Day 5	guidance to follow God's path for your life
Day 6	clear focus
Day 7	for our county to follow God
Day 8	deeper understanding of God's word
Day 9	for a brother/sister in Christ in need
Day 10	for God to reveal anything in your life not pleasing to Him
Day 11	to see yourself as God does
Day 12	to see your situation more clearly
Day 13	to step out in faith
Day 14	to be aware of your divine appointments
Day 15	to better understand someone else's position
Day 16	for an opportunity to bring joy to someone else
17	for God to expose where you have veered off the correct path
18	to deepen your relationship with God
19	to tell someone else something you have learned from God
20	to find simple ways to better enjoy life
21	For courage & opportunity to share God with your family
22	to recognize God for delivering you from a difficult time
23	For courage to follow wherever God leads
24	a deeper desire to spend time with God
25	to not put off what needs to be done
26	to put God in a place of honor in your life so others see Him, not me
27	to stand strong against the enemy
28	to recognize the true enemy
29	to walk in a manner honoring to God
30	to shine Gods light into someone's darkness
31	to maintain perspective of this temporary home

How to Use Your Prayer Journal

Scripture: Ask God to reveal a scripture to pray or select one from your Bible Reading. Write it out here.

Praise: This section of prayer time is all about God.

Begin your prayer time by praising God for who He is. Pray scripture back to Him which is giving Him praise and honor—Psalm is a good source for these scriptures. Acknowledge the ways you have seen God working in your life or in the lives of others.

For Others: This next section of prayer time is devoted to others.

Keep a list of names and their needs, update God in your prayer time. Petition God on behalf of your friends and family just as if you were talking to a friend for them. This type of prayer is called intercessory prayer—you are interceding with God on their behalf.

For Me: This time with God, talk to Him about your personal needs.

Physical, spiritual, emotional, anything. Open up, ve honest, He knows your heart anyway. Talk to Him about your day, your relationships, your challenges, your hopes, your everything.

Prayer isn't about withdrawing from God like an ATM, but rather building a relationship.

Thanksgiving: Lastly, close out your prayer time with thanksgiving.

Everything is from God, so acknowledge Him for all He has provided. Large and small, physical and spiritual, everything comes from Him.

Prayer Journal

Date:

Scripture:

Praise:

For Others:

For Me:

Thanksgiving:

Date:

Scripture:

Praise:

For Others:

For Me:

Thanksgiving:

Date:

Scripture:

Praise:

For Others:

For Me:

Thanksgiving:

Date:

Scripture:

Praise:

For Others:

For Me:

Thanksgiving:

things to Remember

> Remember who you are and *who* you represent.
> — Donna Fender

> The world doesn't change, but we can have confidence to face life's challenges by *trusting* God.
> — Cathy Chung

> Jesus fills up our emptiness and makes us a new *creation*
> — Tara Blake Hatton

> God brings us out of the dark pit and into His *light*.
> — Jana Kennedy-Spicer

> *God* provides true light, even in the darkest of places.
> — Jennifer Cardinal

> The more we get to know God through His Word, the brighter the *light shines*
> — Betsy Jordan Phillips

> The Jesus inside of me is *stronger* than the darkness that threatens to overtake me.
> — Lauren Gaskill

> Our eyes are the window to our whole body. What we see has a lasting effect.
> — Missy Millspaugh

> Lord, create in me a desire for Your *Word*.
> — Jana Kennedy-Spicer

> It is God who keeps our lamp burning, sustaining us in difficult times, helping us bear up under adversity.
> — Gretchen Fleming

God's character of being light is what reveals all of
the pieces of our life, because He alone is the truth.

Terry Holmes

Scripture is: Verse after verse and example after example of God's love for me.

Mitzi Neely

Jesus gives us the Holy Spirit so we can do exceedingly more in His power than in our own strength.

Anne B Say

Prayer and Bible Study can flip a *light switch* on in a dark room.

Jodie Barrett

We need to remember God's *faithfulness* when we are wondering through the darkness.

Adrienne Terrebonne

We can learn a better way of responding to life by looking to the *fountain* of life.

Gretchen Fleming

For many of our loved ones
we will be the greatest access to Jesus they have.

Tara Blake Hatton

Let's proclaim to those around us, the greatness of the God who *loves us.*

Michelle Nietert

God's forgiveness is life-giving, transforming, liberating and it brings us out into *the Light.*

Jana Kennedy-Spicer

> The path, the way, may be unfamiliar to us, but it isn't to God. He is leading us and our role is to *trust Him.*
>
> — Lauren Clark

> A little *light* made all of the difference. Fear left when I could see my way.
>
> — Betsy deCruz

> Your darkest pit is not deeper than God's love for you.
>
> — Becky McCoy

> Walking with Jesus *illuminates* our path and eliminates uncertainty.
>
> — Amanda Wells

> Let's *shine* our light so others can see God.
>
> — Jana Kennedy-Spicer

> Even though there is evil masked as good, God is always good.
>
> — Kristin Funston

> Dear one, God made you one of a kind and loves you *just the way* you are.
>
> — Tina Gibson

> *God showed me* the measure to which He can use me is directly proportional to how open my hands are.
>
> — Lindsey Alexander

> In heaven, God's glory will shine like a *radiant* jewel.
>
> — Jana Kennedy-Spicer

Scripture works like a springboard for prayer.

Betsy deCruz

As spectacular as a sunrise can be, it pales in comparison to the coming *Splendor* of God's Kingdom.

Patti Selvey

To be acquainted with *the light* we must first know who is the light.

We must get to know Jesus. We must get to know God's Word.

Jana Kennedy-Spicer

Darkness hates the light of gratitude. But oh how our Father *loves the light!*

Mitzi Neely

Things to Remember

Things to Remember

meet our Contributors

Soul Friends Walking God's Path Together

Lindsay Alexander's greatest passion is to share the hope and power of Jesus where women not only fully grasp the Gospel but live it out. Through her writing, speaking and singing Lindsay finds ways to encourage women to see their greater purpose in the kingdom and take steps to be all that God created them to be. She has been married for ten years to her college sweetheart Monty and is the mother of three blonde-haired and blue eyed, wide-open and spirited children. She currently lives in South Carolina.
Connect with her at www.lindsayalexanderblog.com

Jodie Barrett is a wife, mother of two teens, speaker, teacher and blogger. Her passion is teaching women the Word of God to help motivate and encourage them to strengthen their faith walk. She looks for joy in the everyday things like laundry, waiting in line and cooking, considering each an opportunity to share God's love with others.

To read more visit Jodie at faithfullyfollowingministries.org

Jennifer Cardinal lives in Bethel, CT with her husband and 13 year old son . She also has two grown college age daughters spreading their wings out in the world. Jen as she known by her friends practiced as a chiropractor for 17 years before moving to CT from NV where she started working for her church in ministry. She loves to write, all things food, and being out in nature whether it's skiing, bike riding, backpacking, kayaking or exploring with her family. She is a self proclaimed imperfect mess who God has rescued and her life now has become a journey in getting to know Him more and more.

Cathy Chung loves Jesus and wants others to love Him too. She has taught the Bible to adults and teens for more than 15 years. Her blog, Seeds of Scripture, encourages readers to grow into a deeper relationship with Him through scripture. She loves gardening, hiking and reading. Cathy is married with three nearly grown children and lives near Boston.

Connect with Cathy at SeedsofScripture.com

Lauren Clark lives in Dallas, Texas, where she moved 5 years ago to be closer to family and help plant a church (Shoreline Dallas). She has been married to Sean Clark for over seven years and they have six dogs and one horse. Lauren's passion is sharing God's love for us through personal stories and relating them to practical Biblical truths that bring life, love, freedom, and encouragement to every area of our lives.

Connect with Lauren at www.laurenjoyclark.com

Betsy de Cruz enjoys God, life with teenagers, and dark roast coffee. She and her family live in the Middle East. Most days she feels privileged to live overseas; other days she wants to pull her hair out and catch the next plane home. Betsy's passion is to encourage women to get God's Word in, so their faith can spill out, even during life's bumpy moments.

You can find Betsy at her blog, faithspillingover.com

Donna Fender is a daughter of the King, wife to an ordained youth pastor, mother of three beautiful children and a physical therapist. Donna loves to sing and loves to find a song for your favorite verse.

To read more visit Donna at faithfullyfollowingministries.org

Gretchen Fleming's passion is to follow hard after Jesus, knowing He is the treasure of a lifetime and worth every minute she commits to Him. She is a Bible study writer, teacher, blogger, and speaker who loves to see Jesus change lives as He's changed hers. It's a joy for her to share with others the Truth that can give perspective and perseverance, no matter what we face.

Join her community at gretchenfleming.com for her blog and Bible study.

Kristin Funston is a little bit of the South and the Southwest rolled into one. A freelance writer and website developer, she works to encourage women to experience and embrace God's Truth amidst the everyday mayhem.

She blogs regularly at KristinFunston.com and MemphisMomsBlog.com.

Lauren Gaskill is an author, blogger and speaker who is passionate about inspiring others to lead joyful, healthy, redeemed lives. She believes life should be sweet — rich in stories, and full of good food, love, encouragement and inspiration. Lauren is the creator of MakingLifeSweet.com and the Finding Joy podcast, and she is in the process of publishing her first inspirational book. When she's not writing, Lauren is creating new recipes in the kitchen or spending time outdoors with her husband and Cavalier King Charles Spaniel.

Tina Gibson has always loved words. Her sweet mom would happily proclaim "She could talk before she could walk!" After a successful career in marketing, Tina has come full circle. Her heart is overflowing with life stories. Tina's joy is to shine for Jesus and share His amazing grace with others. Tina loves taking pictures of the sky, encouraging another soul, and dancing in the living room with her husband, Frank, who inspires her more than he'll ever know.

Connect with Tina on her blog at ww.tinasavantgibson.com

Tara Blake Hatton is a mama, a wife, a teacher, a sister, a daughter, and most importantly a follower of Jesus and a child of God. She has two little boys who love to run and jump and yell and scream and seem to love being attached to their Mama. She has also been blessed with a "bonus" child, stepdaughter Kaleigh, who just turned 12 and does her best to tolerate the antics of her little brothers.

Connect with Tara on her blog at: www.storyofmyheart.org

Terry Holmes is a loyal fan of the 80's, Terry grew up partly in NJ and partly in PA. She is licensed in Elementary and Special Education and taught first grade until becoming a stay-at-home mom to her 3 children. Her desire to speak and write first developed during her years as a mentor mom in MOPS.

Terry is passionate about God's restoration and communicates from her personal experience as a trauma survivor.

Jana Kennedy Spicer is a wife, mom and Nana who is passionate about inspiring and encouraging women on their daily walk with Christ. A woman rescued and repaired by the grace of God, she loves to share about the realness of God's love, redemption and faithfulness. Embarking on a new life journey, she is dedicated to using her blogging, Bible teaching, writing, photography, drawing, painting and graphic designs to bring glory to the Lord.

You can connect with Jana on her blog at SweetToTheSoul.com

Becky L McCoy lives on the Connecticut coast with her two precocious and hilarious children. She once enjoyed teaching high school physics and now tells her story of loss, grief, and joyful living on her blog. Having struggled with depression and anxiety and experienced several seasons of grief and struggle, Becky is passionate about creating an online community where people share their stories and encourage one another to choose to live bravely and authentically at BeckyLMcCoy.com and her podcast Stories of Unfolding Grace.

Missy Millspaugh was born in sunny Florida and lived there until shortly after she married her husband Jim. Since then, they have lived in Texas and she truly believes she was born to be a Texan. Missy has two amazing children, Molly and Jacob and enjoys watching them take their first steps into adulthood. She loves to read, Starbucks, and Mickey Mouse and longs for a house strategically planted in the city, country, and on the beach, all at the same time.

You can connect with Missy at missymillspaugh.com

Mitzi Neely is an inspiring motivational speaker who encourages women of all ages through her experiences and shortcomings. She has been blessed with a passion and love for people that stretches across the generations. Her heart is to lighten your load, while conveying her message that nobody's perfect. Whatever your struggle or need, you will find encouragement through her words as she refreshes your heart and renews your joy.

Follow Mitzi at www.peacefullyimperfect.net.

Michelle Nietert, Licensed Professional Counselor and Clinical Director of Community Counseling Associates has been equipping audiences in the community, church, school and private practice office setting for over twenty years. A happily married mom of two children, Michelle loves inspiring readers and audiences alike to discover Solutions for Life with Practical Teaching and Biblical Wisdom.

Connect with Michelle on her blog at www.counselorthoughts.com

Betsy Jordan Phillips and her family have served in missions for over twenty years. She's gratefully done life, marriage, motherhood and ministry in five different countries. Based in Georgia at the moment, writing lets her continue to share her love for God and His Word across borders.

Connect with Betsy on her blog www.providentiallypunctuated.com

Anne B Say is a natural encourager. Over several decades Anne has traveled throughout the United States, Europe, and parts of Central America. She has been a single mom and a teacher, and understands the challenges of balancing work and home in a pressure-filled world. Her passion is to help others find freedom, peace, and experience all the goodness that life has to offer.

Connect with Anne on her blog at www.annebsay.com

Patti Selvey is a wife and mom of five from Wheaton, IL. She is a full-time graduate student at Moody Theological Seminary (Chicago). A Bible teacher with a shepherd's heart, she loves sharing God's Word with His girls. Patti enjoys all things creative, especially music, writing and photography.

For more of Patti's work visit www.pattiselvey.com.

Adrienne Cooper Terrebonne lives in Valdosta, GA, with her husband and three children. She is a lover of all things chocolate, a recovering people-pleaser, and loves to encourage other moms in their journey of discovering Christ in the chaos.

You can connect with her on her blog at www.blessedbeyondexhaustion.com.

Amanda Wells is the proud wife of a third-generation farmer, and they have taken Psalm 127:5 literally, raising their quiverful of six kids on the farm. She loves baking, reading, writing, and arithmetic (kidding!).

Amanda writes about faith, homeschooling on the farm, and family life at farmwyfe.com.

Index by Author

Lindsey Alexander
Stuck on the Bathroom Floor — 180

Jodie Barrett
Flip on The Light Switch — 96

Jennifer Cardinal
The True Light of God — 32

Cathy Chung
What's This World Coming To — 13

Lauren Clark
Actively Trusting — 142

Betsy DeCruz
When You Need A Light in the Darkness — 148
Bonus Section: Praying Scripture — 201

Donna Fender
The Choice is Yours — 1

Gretchen Fleming
Finding Redemption in the Light — 70
Finding Perspective in God's Light — 121

Kristin Funston
Not Invited to the Party — 174

Lauren Gaskill
No Turning Back — 51

Tina Gibson
Practically Perfect in Every Way — 186

Tara Blake Hatton
No Longer Formless and Empty — 26
A Light Simply Shines — 130

Terry Holmes
Seen by God — 90

Jana Kennedy–Spicer
Introduction ... x
Color Sheet—Matthew 5:14 ... xii
Out of the Pit, Into the Light ... 7
A New Wardrobe ... 19
Bible Study —Word Study ... 24
Color Sheet—Shine so other see Christ ... 38
Brought Out Into the Light ... 57
Color Sheet—Let Your Light Shine ... 63
Bible Study —Bible Study Tools ... 88
No Longer The Rebel ... 102
Color Sheet—Psalm 119:105 ... 114
Bible Study —Verse Mapping ... 126
Color Sheet—John 12:36 ... 154
Be The Light ... 161
Color Sheet—John 1:5 ... 167
Color Sheet—Candle Light ... 192
No More Darkness ... 193
Bonus Section: Praying Scripture ... 201

Becky McCoy
Looking for the Light ... 168

Missy Millspaugh
Be Careful Little Eyes What You See ... 64

Mitzi Neely
God's Redeeming Grace Makes the Difference ... 76
This Little Light of Mine ... 109

Michelle Nietert
Chosen to Proclaim His Excellence ... 136

Betsy Jordan Phillips
No Longer Scared of the Dark ... 45

Anne B Say
Made to be a Light ... 82

Patti Selvey
Pale by Comparison ... 39

Adrienne Terrebonne
Wondering Through the Darkness ... 115

Amanda Wells
Walk in the Light ... 155

additional Resources

Additional Resources

Dive deeper into God's Word with the **Soul Deep Scripture Journal**. A 62-page journal with two full pages of space to journal for each of the *Let Your Light Shine* scriptures.

The Scripture page includes 5 sections:
- Read: the day's scripture
- Reflect: what does this scripture mean
- Relate: how do I apply this scripture to my life
- Pray: talk to God about the scripture and topic
- Remember: what is the day's key take-a-way

The Verse Mapping page includes plenty of room to map out all of the words and phrases of the day's scripture.

Free gifts for you!

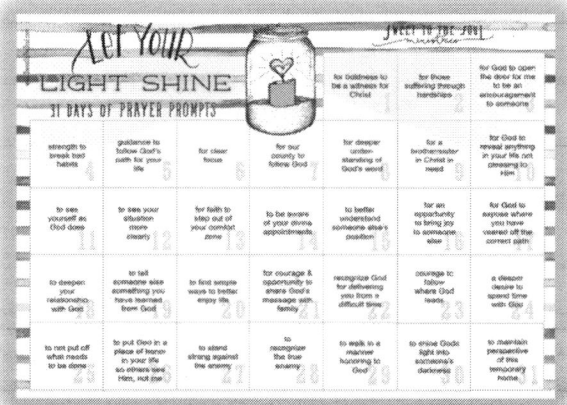

Incorporate prayer into your Soul Deep *Let Your Light Shine* study time with our **31 Days of Prayer Prompts**. Download your printable calendar with 31 daily prayer prompts aligned with the daily scripture.

Blank Scripture Journal Pages & Daily Reading List. One of our goals in developing the Soul Deep materials is to create resources engaging to use if you have a few minutes or if you have hours. Another goal was to make these materials available for little to no cost. To that end, even if you can not invest in a Soul Deep Devotional or Soul Deep Scripture Journal, we want you to invest in spending time in God's Word.

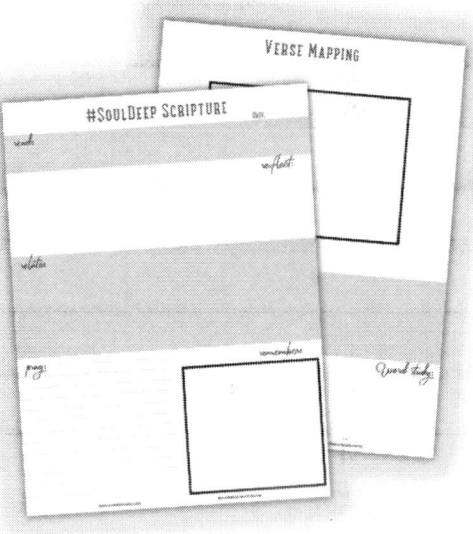

Creative souls who love coloring in their Bibles will enjoy our **Bible Journaling Page Templates**. Whether a novice or a pro, these templates are super easy to use. Print and use as a color sheet or transfer the design into your Journaling Bible. But beware, download these free printables and you'll be hooked!

Visit www.SweetToTheSoul.com to access all of our Soul Deep resources.

Soul Deep Books

Finding New Life in Christ

Check out our full line of **Soul Deep Scripture Journals.**

Dive in to God's Word with each of our 31-day Daily Scripture Reading plans. Designed to allow the user to spend time studying the Bible at their own pace. Use the Scripture Journals daily or at your own preferred scheudle. Spend 10 minutes or 2 hours.

Visit our website to access topical Soul Deep devos on our blog and see the full line of related accessories like scripture cards and Bible Journaling supplies.

Visit www.SweetToTheSoul.com\SoulDeepBooks to access all of our Soul Deep resources.

You Are God's Masterpiece

31 Days of Grace

Soul Deep Books

Learning What Love Is

I Believe : What Do You Believe?

Also available are our **FREE** 7-Day **Soul Deep Mini-Series Scripture Journals**.

Together We're Better

Rest For The Weary Soul

Join our Community

At **Sweet To The Soul Ministries**, we love interacting with our community of beautiful Soul Friends. And if you are not already part of this community, we would love to invite you to join us!

On **Facebook**:
Ministry page:
www.facebook.com/Sweet.To.The.Soul.Ministries
Soul Friends group:
www.facebook.com/groups/SweetToTheSoulFriends/
Prayer Closet group:
www.facebook.com/groups/SweetToTheSoulPrayerCloset/

On **Instagram**:
www.instagram.com/jana_sweettothesoul/

On **Twitter**:
twitter.com/_SweetToTheSoul

On **Pinterest**:
www.pinterest.com/sweettothesoul/

Visit our Shoppe

On **Etsy**:
www.etsy.com/shop/SweetToTheSoulShoppe

On **Instagram**:
www.instagram.com/sweettothesoulshoppe/

Made in the USA
Middletown, DE
08 August 2018